WRAPS
AND
ROLL-UPS

Revised Edition

Dona Z. Meilach

BRISTOL PUBLISHING ENTERPRISES

Hayward, California

A **nitty gritty**® cookbook.

©2005 Bristol Publishing Enterprises, 2714 McCone Ave., Hayward, CA 94545.

Printed in the United States of America.

ISBN 1-55867-307-5

Cover design: Frank J. Paredes
Cover photography: John A. Benson
Food styling: Randy Mon
Illustrations: Shanti Nelson

CONTENTS

To Mel, Susan and Allen

MOVE OVER, SANDWICH!

Move over sandwich! Look out burrito! You are being replaced! There is a new sibling in the family with genetic elements of both — the wrap.

What is a wrap? It is a tortilla, lavosh or other flatbread folded around enough goodies to be a complete meal. By comparison, the sandwich is limited in content and appeal, unable to hold the same variety and quantity of ingredients as a wrap. The burrito, on the other hand, is limited by the small range of ingredients that make it authentic. In a wrap, the ingredients are "anything goes."

Although wraps reportedly started in the South, they went multicultural and mainstream when upscale fast-food wrap restaurants began to pop up all over Northern California. These restaurants offered a menu of overstuffed tortillas with such international ingredients as Thai chicken, teriyaki steak, barbecued prawns and sautéed duck, all wrapped up with rice, vegetables, salads, cheeses, nuts, exotic salsas and sauces. Soon, fine dining establishments and chain restaurants began offering variations of wraps. Now they're even available in the frozen food section of many supermarkets.

What is the wrap's appeal? Mainly, it's that it can contain a full meal, and that its contents are limited only by your imagination. Packaged in foil or parchment paper, you can tote a wrap down the street, nibble on one at a café table or, when desperate, tackle a wrap in your car while driving. A wrap can be cut in half and served elegantly on a plate and eaten with a knife and fork. Wraps are also quite filling. Some are so big that you can take half home for dinner or share it with your significant other.

A roll-up, a relative of the wrap, can contain the same multitude of ingredients as a wrap. The fillings are rolled up in the tortilla, lavosh or other flatbread jelly roll-style. After a period of refrigeration, the roll is cut into 1- to 1½-inch rounds, revealing a pinwheel of filling inside. Roll-ups are commonly served cold as savory appetizers, but 2 or 3 pieces could be a satisfying meal.

Some restaurant wraps weigh as much as a pound and can tally up 1000 calories. If the fillings are cooked in butter and oil, wrapped in a lard-based tortilla and covered in high-fat dressing, carumba! — you'll eat more fat calories in one meal than the recommended day's allowance. When you make your own wraps you can control their content and size.

The key to success when making your own wraps is to make or buy your favorite ingredients and assemble them creatively. Within the "anything goes" philosophy, if you maintain a proper balance of foods and avoid those that are dripping in fat or laden with calories, you can create a healthy and satisfying meal. Following are suggestions for mix-and-match ingredients.

MAKING YOUR OWN WRAPS AND ROLL-UPS

MAIN FILLINGS

Choose your favorite food to serve as the star in your homemade wraps and roll-ups. Beef, lamb, pork, chicken, turkey, duck, fish, shellfish and a variety of vegetables are all fair game. Marinate your ingredients for extra flavor. Then, sauté, stir-fry, bake, grill, broil or steam them.

BINDERS

Binders are used to hold ingredients together and to give the wrap solidity.

Choose rice, couscous, orzo, quinoa or other types of grains. Experiment with different rice, such as jasmine, basmati, brown and wild rice.

Beans are also a good binder, and are a typical ingredient in burrito-style wraps. Other types of legumes are suitable as well. Choose lentils, pinto beans, garbanzo beans, refried beans, black beans, red kidney beans, white beans and any number of others that suit your taste.

Potatoes and squash are interesting choices for binders and are popular on many wrap restaurant menus. Choose diced or mashed white or sweet potatoes, or even cubes of squash.

CRUNCH

Crunch is an important taste-texture sensation for wraps and roll-ups. Choose crisp fresh vegetables, salad greens, cole slaw, nuts or sunflower kernels.

FLAVORINGS

In addition to salsa, a variety of sauces can flavor wraps. Salad dressings, barbecue sauce, chili sauce, Thai peanut sauce, Indian chutney, hoisin sauce, teriyaki sauce and pesto are only some of the choices. Don't forget sour cream, guacamole and chile peppers for traditional flavor. Other flavorings include lime and lemon juice, flavored oils and vinegars, fresh ginger and a multitude of herbs and spices.

COLD, WARM OR HOT?

- Serve wraps cold if they contain salads only. Roll-ups are served cold.
- Serve wraps slightly tepid if they contain salads, rice, poultry, meat or fish.
- Wraps can be served warm if you prefer. Heat oven to 325° or 350°. Enclose wrap in aluminum foil and heat in oven for about 5 to 10 minutes. Wraps can also be warmed in the microwave, but not if wrapped in aluminum foil.

WRAPPING IT ALL UP

There is no right or wrong way to fold a wrap. Choose the best method for the occasion.

ENVELOPE-STYLE

Lay the wrapper flat. Spoon filling onto the lower third of the wrapper. Fold the sides in towards the center. Fold the bottom edge up towards the center. Gently, but tightly, roll up to the top flap. If desired, wrap securely with aluminum foil or sandwich paper using the same method. Tear off or fold back the foil as you eat. Or, place the wrap on a plate, seam-side down, and cut in half crosswise.

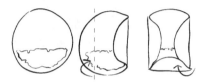

EAT-AND-RUN-STYLE

Lay the wrapper flat. Spoon filling onto the lower third of the wrapper. Fold the right edge in toward the center. Fold the bottom edge up toward the center. Gently, but tightly, roll up to the top flap. The left end is left open for nibbling, ice-cream-cone style. If desired, wrap securely with aluminum foil or sandwich paper using the same method. Tear off or fold back the foil as you eat.

DAINTY EATER-STYLE

Lay the wrapper flat. Spoon filling onto the center of the wrapper and roll up jelly roll-fashion; the ends remain open. Serve this on a plate and eat it with a knife and fork.

ROLL-UP-STYLE

Spread cheese, yogurt or other spreadable ingredient over the entire wrapper all the way to the ends. Layer thinly sliced fillings, striving for color and texture contrast, over the wrapper. Roll up tightly, jelly roll-style, into a log. Wrap with plastic wrap, waxed paper or aluminum foil and twist ends to secure. Refrigerate for 1 to 4 hours, until firm. Unwrap the log and slice it into 1- to 1½-inch rounds with a sharp knife. Serve as a finger food for appetizers, lunches or other meals.

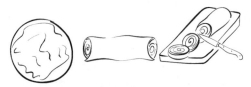

SERVING WRAPS AND ROLL-UPS

There are as many ways to serve wraps as there are ingredients to fill them.

In Your Hand: Cover wrap with aluminum foil or sandwich paper to keep your hands clean. Keep wrap whole or cut in half. As you eat, peel away enough of the foil to take a couple of bites. Continue peeling as you eat.

On a Plate: Cut the wrap in half at an angle. Stand one half upright on the plate and place the other half on its side. Optionally, lay the wrap on the plate and sprinkle with chopped fresh chives, parsley or cilantro. Or, pipe a decorative line of sour cream along the top of the wrap. Accompany with a green salad or a fruit salad.

On a Platter: Place roll-up rounds flat on a pretty serving platter to reveal the pinwheel of filling. If serving roll-ups as appetizers with other items, count on about 2 to 3 rounds per person.

Do It Yourself: Present a variety of wrap ingredients on a buffet table. Show guests how to assemble and wrap their own.

WRAPPERS

TRENDY WRAPPERS

Tortillas, lavosh and pita breads are popular "wrappers" for today's wraps. Each is easy to make at home, but is also available ready-made. All begin as balls of dough that are flattened and fried on a griddle or baked. Wrappers must be kept soft to be flexible enough to enclose the fillings.

In general, flour tortillas, made from white or whole wheat flour, are favored over corn tortillas for making wraps. Wheat flour provides more "stretch" than cornmeal. Flour tortillas can be flavored variously with such things as spinach, tomatoes, basil, cilantro, black pepper, fresh ginger, garlic, salsa and cheese. You can also make tortillas in dessert flavors, such as strawberry, banana, cinnamon-apple and chocolate.

Experienced tortilla makers hand-stretch balls of dough into flat rounds. Most home bakers shape tortillas with a rolling pin. You can also use a special tool called a tortilla press, which can be found in specialty housewares stores, but these models usually only make 6-inch tortillas. A tortilla that holds a healthy amount of filling should be 10 to 16 inches in diameter.

LETTUCE WRAPS

Replace tortillas, pita and lavosh with lettuce: the latest wrap for any variety of foods. Lettuce wraps take their cue from Asian cuisine where "lettuce parcels" are a time-honored dish. Lettuce wraps represent "fusion" cooking, fusing the food of one nation with food from another. Asian cookbooks, and especially those from Thailand, offer a mouth-watering assortment of fillings for the curled leaves of iceberg lettuce. Often, the same ingredients are wrapped with a tortilla. Any of the recipes usually wrapped in a tortilla can also be served in lettuce leaves. In answer to the low-carb meals touted by diet plans, many fast food restaurants are now offering to put any sandwich, from hamburgers to fish fillets, in lettuce for the asking. So take your cue from Asian cuisine and develop fusion recipes for wraps and roll-ups from the recipes here or from your own creative food combinations. We have included a new 'Lettuce Wraps' section in this revision of the book, just to get you started.

MAKING TORTILLAS

The following tortilla recipes are composed of 4 major components: dry ingredients, fat, liquid and additional flavorings. The amount of liquid can vary by a spoonful or two, depending on the moisture in the air. Traditionally, tortillas are made with lard, but butter, vegetable shortening and vegetable oil can be substituted. Try a few of the recipes here; then, improvise using your favorite flavorings. Don't be afraid — tortilla making is easy and forgiving.

Mixing Tortillas by Hand: In a medium bowl, mix dry ingredients until blended. With a fork, cut in fat until mixture is thoroughly mixed and has a coarse texture. Add about ⅓ of the liquid at a time, mixing until a large soft mass forms; add more liquid, if necessary. Gather dough into a ball, add flavorings, if using, and knead 15 to 20 times in bowl until a soft dough forms. If sticky, add a little more flour.

Mixing Tortillas with a Food Processor: Combine dry ingredients and fat in a food processor workbowl and process for about 2 minutes, until coarse crumbs form. Add liquid ⅓ at a time and process until mixture forms a soft mass around the blade (about 30 seconds). Add flavorings, if using, just as dough is forming a ball. Remove dough carefully and knead gently on a board 15 to 20 times.

Shaping Tortillas: Divide dough into pieces, depending upon the size desired.
Most of the wraps in this book use large tortillas.

- 4 pieces for large tortillas (14 to 16 inches)
- 6 pieces for medium tortillas (10 to 12 inches)
- 12 pieces for small tortillas (8 inches)

Roll each dough piece into a smooth ball. Place balls on a clean dishtowel, cover with another clean dishtowel or plastic wrap and let rest for 20 minutes. On a lightly floured surface, flatten 1 dough ball. With a rolling pin, gently roll dough from the center outward, turning it over once or twice, until about ⅛-inch thick and desired diameter. Cook tortilla following the directions below. Repeat with remaining dough balls, cooking as each tortilla is made. As you become skilled at making tortillas, consider making square or rectangle-shaped tortillas for easier wrapping.

Cooking Tortillas: Heat a heavy, smooth-surfaced nonstick skillet or griddle over medium heat. Cook each tortilla for about 45 to 60 seconds, or until blistered and lightly browned on one side. Flip tortilla and cook on the opposite side for 1 to 2 minutes. Cool on a wire rack, stacking tortillas. Cool stack for about 5 minutes and use immediately. Or, place tortillas in a locking plastic bag while still warm; this will keep them flexible.

STORING AND REHEATING TORTILLAS

Store purchased tortillas in locking plastic bags or wrapped in aluminum foil. Store homemade tortillas in locking plastic bags. All tortillas can be kept refrigerated for a week or so, or frozen flat for up to 6 months.

REHEATING TORTILLAS

Microwave: Sprinkle water on 2 paper towels and place 1 tortilla between towels. Heat 4 to 5 layers of tortillas on MEDIUM for about 1 minute; heat individual tortillas for about 30 seconds. Or, place 2 to 3 tortillas in an open plastic storage bag and heat for ½ to 1 minute on LOW.

Steam: Cook tortillas in a steamer basket over simmering water for a few seconds on each side.

Bake: Heat oven to 350°. Wrap 3 to 4 tortillas with aluminum foil or parchment paper and bake for 5 to 8 minutes, until warm.

Fry: Heat a skillet over medium heat until hot. Place tortillas, one at a time, in skillet and cook for about 30 seconds on each side.

Grill: Lay tortillas flat on a hot grill for a few seconds, flipping over and quickly removing from heat. The timing will depend on the temperature of the fire and distance of tortilla from the heat source.

BASIC FLOUR TORTILLAS

Begin with this recipe. Once perfected, use any or all of the flavored variations.

DRY INGREDIENTS
2½ cups all-purpose flour
1½ tsp. baking powder
1 tsp. salt

FAT
2 tbs. softened unsalted butter, vegetable shortening, vegetable oil or lard

LIQUID
about ¾ cup lukewarm water

Follow instructions on pages 10 to 12 for mixing, shaping and cooking tortillas.

SPINACH TORTILLAS

These tortillas have a wonderful green color and are especially pretty wrapped around fillings with contrasting colors. For an even greener color, add a scant drop of green food coloring to the water.

DRY INGREDIENTS
2½ cups all-purpose flour
1½ tsp. baking powder
1 tsp. salt

FAT
2 tbs. softened unsalted butter, vegetable shortening, vegetable oil or lard

LIQUID
about ¾ cup lukewarm water

ADDITIONAL FLAVORINGS
½ cup finely minced fresh spinach leaves

Follow instructions on pages 10 to 12 for mixing, shaping and cooking tortillas.

TOMATO TORTILLAS

The tomato yields a subtle color and wonderful taste. A drop or two of red food coloring added to the water will enhance the color.

DRY INGREDIENTS

2½ cups all-purpose flour   1 tsp. salt
1½ tsp. baking powder

FAT

2 tbs. softened unsalted butter, vegetable shortening, vegetable oil or lard
¼ cup tomato paste*

LIQUID

about ¾ cup lukewarm water

ADDITIONAL FLAVORINGS

Follow instructions on pages 10 to 12 for mixing, shaping and cooking tortillas. Mix or pulse for an extra minute until mixture is evenly colored.

*Although tomato paste doesn't contain fat, it is treated as fat for mixing purposes in this recipe.

SUN-DRIED TOMATO TORTILLAS

These light-red, flecked tortillas look as good as they taste. To reconstitute sun-dried tomatoes, soak them in very hot water for 30 minutes; drain well before using.

DRY INGREDIENTS
2½ cups all-purpose flour
1½ tsp. baking powder
1 tsp. salt
6 dry sun-dried tomatoes, reconstituted and finely minced

FAT
2 tbs. softened unsalted butter, vegetable shortening, vegetable oil or lard

LIQUID
about ⅞ cup lukewarm milk

ADDITIONAL FLAVORINGS
none

Follow instructions on pages 10 to 12 for mixing, shaping and cooking tortillas.

HERB AND CHILI TORTILLAS

Specks of green herbs and red chili powder dot this pretty tortilla. Use cilantro, basil or parsley.

DRY INGREDIENTS
2½ cups all-purpose flour
1½ tsp. baking powder
1 tsp. salt

FAT
2 tbs. softened unsalted butter, vegetable shortening, vegetable oil or lard

LIQUID
about ¾ cup lukewarm water

ADDITIONAL FLAVORINGS
1 tbs. chili powder
2 tbs. finely chopped fresh herbs

Follow instructions on pages 10 to 12 for mixing, shaping and cooking tortillas.

BLACK PEPPER AND
GREEN CHILE TORTILLAS

Adjust the heat of this tortilla by reducing or increasing the amount of chiles used.

DRY INGREDIENTS

2½ cups all-purpose flour, or more if needed   1 tsp. salt

1½ tsp. baking powder   1 tbs. black pepper

FAT

2 tbs. softened unsalted butter, vegetable shortening, vegetable oil or lard

LIQUID

about ¾ cup lukewarm water

1 can (4 oz.) chopped green chiles with a small amount of the chile liquid

ADDITIONAL FLAVORINGS

Follow instructions on pages 10 to 12 for mixing, shaping and cooking tortillas. Add flour as needed if the dough gets too moist.

WHOLE WHEAT FLOUR TORTILLAS

Makes 4 large or 6 medium tortillas

For a slightly stronger wheat flavor, use all whole wheat flour.

DRY INGREDIENTS
1½ cups whole wheat flour
1 cup unbleached all-purpose flour
½ tsp. salt
2 tsp. baking powder

FAT
2 tbs. vegetable oil

LIQUID
¾ cup plus 1–2 tbs. water

ADDITIONAL FLAVORINGS
none

Follow instructions on pages 10 to 12 for mixing, shaping and cooking tortillas.

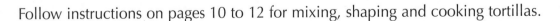

STRAWBERRY TORTILLAS

Makes 4 large or 6 medium tortillas

Fruit-flavored tortillas are ideal for desserts. The light pink color of this tortilla can be intensified with a drop of red food coloring, if desired.

DRY INGREDIENTS

2½ cups all-purpose flour   1 tsp. salt
1½ tsp. baking powder

FAT

2 tbs. softened unsalted butter, vegetable shortening or vegetable oil

LIQUID

about ½ cup lukewarm water   ¼ cup mashed fresh strawberries

ADDITIONAL FLAVORINGS

Follow instructions on pages 10 to 12 for mixing, shaping and cooking tortillas.

VARIATION: BANANA TORTILLAS

Substitute ¼ cup mashed bananas for strawberries.

CHOCOLATE TORTILLAS

Makes 4 large or 6 medium tortillas

A rich chocolate flavor and toasty color make these ideal dessert tortillas. Fill them with fresh or cooked fruits and whipped cream.

DRY INGREDIENTS

2½ cups all-purpose flour
1½ tsp. baking powder
1 tsp. salt

¼ cup cocoa powder
1 tsp. cinnamon
2 tsp. sugar

FAT

2 tbs. softened unsalted butter

LIQUID

about ¾ cup lukewarm water
1 tbs. vanilla extract

ADDITIONAL FLAVORINGS

Follow instructions on pages 10 to 12 for mixing, shaping and cooking tortillas.

CINNAMON-APPLE TORTILLAS

These tortillas work well with chicken or dessert fillings. For a quick dessert, spread syrup over each tortilla and sprinkle with cinnamon-sugar. Or, spread with jelly and cream cheese.

DRY INGREDIENTS

2½ cups all-purpose flour

¾ tsp. salt

1½ tsp. baking powder

1 tsp. cinnamon

FAT

2 tbs. softened unsalted butter or vegetable oil

LIQUID

¾ cup slightly warm applesauce

about 1 tbs. warm water

ADDITIONAL FLAVORINGS

Follow instructions on pages 10 to 12 for mixing, shaping and cooking tortillas.

CORN TORTILLAS

Makes 5–6 medium tortillas

Masa harina is a special type of cornmeal specifically ground for corn tortillas. It is available in the Mexican food aisle of grocery stores and in Latin American markets.

2 cups masa harina
¼ tsp. salt

1¼ cups warm water

In a medium bowl, mix masa harina and salt. Add 1 cup of the water, a little at a time, until dough holds a shape. Knead in bowl for about 5 minutes, adding more water if necessary, until dough is smooth. Divide dough into 5 to 6 pieces and roll each piece into a smooth ball. Place balls on a clean dishtowel, cover with another clean dishtowel or plastic wrap and let rest for 20 minutes.

On a lightly floured surface, flatten 1 dough ball. With a rolling pin, gently roll dough from the center outward, turning it over once or twice, until about ⅛-inch thick and desired diameter.

To cook tortillas, heat a heavy, smooth-surfaced nonstick skillet or griddle over medium heat. Cook each tortilla for about 45 to 60 seconds, or until blistered and lightly browned on one side. Flip tortilla and cook on the opposite side for 1 to 2 minutes. Cool on a wire rack, stacking tortillas. Use immediately.

LAVOSH

Makes 3–4

Lavosh, or Armenian cracker bread, can be found in soft and crisp versions. Here is a method of making soft lavosh at home. Lavosh must be rolled very thinly and baked for a short period of time so that it stays soft for wrapping. To soften crisp homemade or purchased lavosh, sprinkle it with water and cover it with a towel for a couple of hours.

2½ cups all-purpose flour
1 tsp. white sugar
1 tsp. salt
⅔ cup water

1 egg white
2 tbs. butter, melted
2 egg whites, beaten

Heat oven to 400°. In a large bowl, stir together flour, sugar and salt. Add water, egg white, and melted butter; mix well to make a stiff dough. Knead until dough is smooth, about 5 minutes. Divide dough into 8 balls. Roll each ball on a lightly floured surface until paper-thin and 12 to 14 inches in diameter. Place on an ungreased baking sheet. Brush with egg white. Pierce each circle with the tines of a fork in rows about 1½ inches apart.

Bake in a preheated oven for 5 minutes for soft lavosh; 10 to 12 minutes for crisp lavosh.

POCKETLESS PITA BREADS

Makes 5–6

Pita, a Middle-Eastern flatbread, usually comes with a pocket in the middle for fillings. Here is a variation of pita, which is rolled thin enough so that it doesn't form a pocket while baking. Pocketless pita bread is ideal for wraps.

2 tsp. active dry yeast
1½ cups warm water (about 110°)
½ tsp. salt
2 tbs. olive oil

¾ tsp. sugar
1 cup whole wheat flour
3 cups all-purpose flour or bread flour

In a large bowl, sprinkle yeast over warm water and let stand for about 5 minutes, until foamy. Stir in salt, oil and sugar. Add flours and knead by hand or with a heavy duty mixer until dough is smooth and elastic. Place dough in a lightly oiled bowl, cover with a towel and let rise for about 1 hour, until doubled in size. Punch down dough and let stand for about 5 minutes.

Heat oven to 500°. On a lightly floured board, knead dough lightly for about 1 minute. Cut dough into 5 to 6 equal pieces. With a rolling pin, roll each piece into ⅛-inch-thick 8- to 10-inch round. Place rounds on a greased baking sheet and bake for 5 to 6 minutes, until slightly browned. Cool for 1 minute and store in a large locking plastic bag.

BINDERS

HOLDING IT ALL TOGETHER

Rice is often the ingredient that binds, or holds the other foods together in a fully stuffed wrap. Try different rice varieties such as long-grain, jasmine, basmati, Texmati, brown, wild and combinations of rice. Flavor the rices variously with curry, cumin, saffron, red and green pepper flakes, dried mushrooms, raisins, apricots or other items. Couscous, orzo and quinoa are tasty replacements for rice in a wrap and give it a little ethnic flair.

Beans, too, are excellent binders for wraps. They provide bulk as well as great flavor. For ease, use beans from cans. You can also cook your own dried beans and flavor them in various ways. Dried beans must be soaked prior to cooking. There are two general methods:

Overnight Soak: Soak 1 part dried beans in 3 parts water and refrigerate overnight. Drain beans and cook in fresh cold water.

Quick Soak: Place dried beans in a large pot, cover with cold water and bring to a boil. Remove pot from heat, cover and let beans stand for about 1½ to 2 hours. Drain beans and cook in fresh cold water.

BASIC RICE

Makes 2 cups

The liquid for cooking rice can be water, tomato juice, or chicken, beef or vegetable stock. Experiment with your own flavor combinations. Brown and wild rice require longer cooking times, usually 45 to 50 minutes. A rice cooker is a handy appliance to have around when making wraps. Follow manufacturer's instructions for making rice. This recipe can be increased easily to serve a crowd; just remember the ratio of 1 part rice to 2 parts liquid.

1 cup rice
2 cups liquid

Place rice and liquid in a large saucepan and bring to a boil. Cover pan, reduce heat to very low and simmer for about 15 minutes, until all liquid is absorbed. Remove pan from heat, remove lid and fluff rice with a fork; let stand for about 5 minutes.

VARIATION: CURRIED RICE

In a saucepan, heat 2 tsp. oil over medium-low heat. Add 1 cup rice and 1 to 2 tbs. curry powder and stir until curry is fragrant. Add 2 cups water and continue with recipe instructions.

QUICK SPANISH RICE

This zesty rice blend adds color and flavor to wraps. Serve it in a spinach tortilla with cooked chicken, tuna or ground beef and an array of brightly colored vegetables.

1 cup long-grain white, basmati or jasmine rice
1 cup water
1 can (14.5 oz.) stewed tomatoes
½ tsp. chili powder
1 tsp. salt
⅛ tsp. pepper

In a 3-quart saucepan, bring rice, water and tomatoes to a boil. Add chili powder, salt and pepper, reduce heat to very low and simmer, covered, for about 20 minutes, or until all liquid is absorbed. Remove pan from heat, uncover and fluff rice with a fork; let stand for 5 minutes.

SOUTHWESTERN RICE

Making fresh Southwestern-flavored rice is easy. When you are in a rush, look for packaged Southwestern rice mixes.

1 tbs. butter, oil or margarine
½ cup thinly sliced white onion
1 clove garlic, minced
peel (zest) from 1 lemon
6 white mushrooms, thinly sliced
2 cups water or consommé

½ cup wild rice
½ cup long-grain white rice
¼ cup finely chopped carrot
1 medium-sized red bell pepper, seeded,
   ribs removed and cut into thin strips

In a large saucepan, melt butter over medium heat and sauté onion and garlic until translucent. Add lemon peel and mushrooms and sauté for about 2 minutes. Add water and wild rice and bring to a boil. Reduce heat to low and simmer, covered tightly, for 25 minutes. Stir in white rice, carrot and bell pepper. Simmer, covered tightly, for 20 minutes, or until all liquid is absorbed. Remove pan from heat and let stand for 5 minutes. Uncover pan and fluff grains with a fork.

MIDDLE EASTERN PILAF

The different flavors in this Middle Eastern dish contribute to the international concept of wraps.

1 tbs. vegetable oil
1 small yellow onion, diced
2 tbs. pine nuts
1 cup basmati or other long-grain rice
2 cups chicken stock or water

1 tsp. red pepper flakes
⅓ cup golden raisins
2 tsp. grated fresh lime peel (zest)
½ tsp. cinnamon
1 tsp. blanched slivered almonds, toasted

In a medium saucepan, heat oil over medium heat and sauté onion and pine nuts for about 5 minutes, until onions are soft and nuts are slightly browned. Stir in rice and sauté for 4 to 5 minutes, stirring frequently. Stir in stock, pepper flakes, raisins, lime peel and cinnamon and bring to a boil. Reduce heat to very low, cover, and simmer for about 15 to 18 minutes, until all liquid has been absorbed. Remove pan from heat, uncover and fluff rice with a fork. Stir in almonds.

BASIC COUSCOUS

Couscous, sometimes called "Moroccan pasta" is made from semolina flour, the same hard-wheat flour that is used to make pasta. Purchase instant couscous and it needs no cooking. This recipe is easily increased for a crowd if you keep in mind the ratio of 1 part couscous to 1½ parts liquid. The couscous will almost triple in volume when the liquid is absorbed.

1 cup instant couscous
1½ cups boiling water, or chicken, beef or vegetable stock

In a saucepan or heatproof bowl, mix couscous with boiling water. Cover and let stand for 2 to 3 minutes, until all liquid is absorbed. Uncover pan and fluff grains with a fork.

VARIATION: ORANGE COUSCOUS

In a saucepan, bring 2 cups water and ¼ cup orange juice to a boil. Remove from heat and stir in 1½ cups instant couscous and ½ cup raisins. Cover and let stand for about 3 minutes, until all liquid is absorbed. Uncover pan and fluff grains with a fork.

ORZO

Orzo is a small rice-shaped pasta that cooks just like spaghetti. One cup of dried orzo will expand to about 3 cups when cooked.

1 cup dried orzo
¼ tsp. salt
1 tsp. vegetable oil

Bring a large pot of water to a boil. Add orzo, salt and oil, reduce heat and cook at a low boil for about 10 minutes; drain.

VARIATION: ORZO AND VEGETABLES

This method saves preparation time when you want to serve both orzo and cooked vegetables in your wrap.

Cook ⅓ cup dried orzo in boiling water for about 5 minutes. Add 2 cups chopped vegetables to cooking water. Reduce heat slightly and cook until vegetables are tender and pasta is done, about 10 minutes.

QUINOA

Quinoa is a nutritious, ancient Peruvian staple. Look for it in health food stores. It makes an excellent binder for wraps and is a tasty alternative to rice. To increase the quantity, use a ratio of 1 part quinoa to 3 parts boiling water.

1 cup quinoa
3 cups boiling water

In a saucepan, bring quinoa and water to a boil. Reduce heat to low and simmer, covered, for about 15 minutes, or until liquid is absorbed. Uncover pan and fluff grains with a fork.

SPICY BLACK BEANS

Gently simmering the beans helps to retain their shape. You can flavor them with different herbs and spices to suit your taste.

2 cups black beans, soaked (see page 28) and drained
¼ cup olive oil
3 tbs. fresh lime juice
2 tbs. chopped cilantro
½ tsp. ground cumin

1 medium-sized red or green bell pepper, seeded, ribs removed, diced
½ medium-sized red onion, diced
1 jalapeño chile pepper, seeded and minced, optional
salt and pepper to taste

In a large pot, cover beans with cold water by 2 inches and bring to a boil. Reduce heat to low and simmer for 1½ to 2 hours, until tender. Drain and cool slightly.

In a large bowl, mix oil with lime juice, cilantro and cumin. Add beans, bell pepper, onion, jalapeño, if using, salt and pepper. Toss all ingredients until well blended.

MEXICAN-STYLE PINTO BEANS

Traditionally, pinto beans are flavored with ham, bacon or salt pork during cooking. For a vegetarian version, omit the ham. These beans will be a bit soupy; dish them up with a slotted spoon.

1 lb. dried pinto beans, soaked (see page 28) and drained
1 cup chopped onion
2 cloves garlic, minced
½ cup diced ham, salt pork or bacon
1 tsp. dried oregano
1 can (6 oz.) whole green chiles, seeded and chopped, optional
2 tbs. sugar
½ tsp. salt
¼ cup chopped cilantro, optional

In a large pot, cover beans with cold water by 1 inch. Add onion, garlic, ham, oregano, green chiles and sugar and bring to a boil. Reduce heat to low and simmer for about 2 hours, until tender. Season with salt. If desired, stir in cilantro just before serving.

SALADS AND SLAWS

ADDING CRUNCH TO WRAPS AND ROLL-UPS

Crunch is an important component in wraps. It provides a snappy sensation for the mouth and a healthy amount of nutrition.

A mixture of your favorite crisp vegetables is a good way to add crunch. Consider: cucumber, celery, carrots, cabbage, broccoli, jicama, water chestnuts, bell peppers, radishes, bean sprouts or other items. Many of these items can be found pre-cut in the produce section of the supermarket.

Cole slaw, and variations of it, is a common ingredient on many wrap restaurants menus. Make your own slaw by using blends of different cabbages and tangy salad dressings. Throw in a few shredded vegetables for color. Toss the slaw ingredients with the dressing about an hour before assembling the wrap. Keep in the refrigerator and you will have a nice temperature contrast in the wrap. Drain off the excess liquid before placing in the wrapper.

Crisp tossed green salads are another typical addition to restaurant-style wraps. Consider adding your favorite salad, such as Caesar salad, to the wrap ingredients. Pay attention to the components in the dressing and check to see that their flavors will complement the other ingredients in the wrap.

CLASSIC COLE SLAW

Makes 4 cups

The low-fat dressing in this recipe works well on any type of cole slaw. For variety, replace 1 cup of the cabbage with shredded carrots, chopped red or green bell pepper and/or bean sprouts.

½ cup nonfat plain yogurt or nonfat
   mayonnaise
2 tbs. Dijon-style mustard
2 tbs. white wine vinegar
3-4 cups mixed shredded green and red
   cabbage

½ cup thinly sliced green onions or minced
   white or red onion
salt and pepper to taste

In a large bowl, combine yogurt, mustard and vinegar and whip until smooth. Add cabbage and green onions and toss well. Season with salt and pepper. Refrigerate for about 1 hour before using.

VARIATION: COLE SLAW VINAIGRETTE

Substitute 1 cup *Old-Fashioned Vinaigrette* or *Creamy Vinaigrette*, page 41, for yogurt, mustard and vinegar.

OLD-FASHIONED VINAIGRETTE

This dressing will flavor about 3 cups cole slaw or other vegetables.

1 tsp. salt
¼ tsp. pepper
½ tsp. Dijon-style mustard
2 tbs. sugar

1 tsp. dried minced onion
⅓ cup white wine vinegar
3 tbs. vegetable oil

In a small bowl, add salt, pepper, mustard, sugar and onion and mix well. With a wire whisk, blend in vinegar. Whisking continuously, slowly add oil until well blended.

CREAMY VINAIGRETTE

Use this on virtually any salad or vegetable used in a wrap. Try different flavored vinegars and different flavored oils.

3 tbs. plain, nonfat yogurt or reduced-fat
   sour cream

¼ cup white wine vinegar, or other to taste
2 tbs. vegetable oil

Whisk ingredients together until blended.

MEXICAN SLAW

This traditional Mexican slaw dressing is good with other vegetables, too.

½ cup low-fat plain yogurt
½ tsp. ground cumin
⅛ tsp. salt
freshly ground pepper to taste
3 cups mixed shredded red and green
   cabbage
2 carrots, peeled and grated

In a large bowl, combine yogurt, cumin, salt and pepper and mix well. Add cabbage and carrots and toss well. Refrigerate for about 1 hour before using.

THAI SLAW

A distinctive peanut flavor is perfect for Thai or other Southeast Asian-inspired wraps.

3 cups mixed shredded red and green
   cabbage
2 carrots, peeled and grated

Thai Peanut Sauce, follows
¼ cup peanuts

In a large bowl, mix cabbage and carrots. Add sauce and peanuts and toss until well coated.

THAI PEANUT SAUCE

½ cup creamy peanut butter
½ cup sugar
1 tbs. grated fresh orange peel (zest)

3 tbs. water
1 tsp. ground ginger
2 tbs. vegetable oil

In a small saucepan, combine all ingredients. Cook over low heat, stirring constantly, for about 2 to 3 minutes, until melted and smooth. Cool before using.

CAESAR SALAD

This recipe will add sharp flavors to any wrap. Or, eat it as a side salad with fresh croutons.

1 large head romaine lettuce, torn into bite-sized pieces
Zesty Caesar Dressing, follows

Place lettuce in a large bowl. Add dressing and toss until well coated.

ZESTY CAESAR DRESSING

½ cup mayonnaise
½ cup chicken stock
2 tbs. grated Parmesan cheese
1½ tbs. red wine vinegar
1 hard-cooked egg, quartered

½ tsp. Dijon-style mustard
½ tsp. Worcestershire sauce
⅛ tsp. pepper
4 anchovy fillets, chopped, optional

Process all ingredients with a blender or food processor until smooth. Pour into a jar, cover and chill for at least 1 hour to blend flavors.

SALSAS AND SAUCES

ADDING ZEST TO WRAPS AND ROLL-UPS

Salsa, which means "sauce" in Spanish, is a common ingredient in wraps. Traditional salsa is made with tomatoes or tomatillos, onions, chiles, herbs and spices and comes in varieties from mild to very hot. Today, salsas are made from a variety of fruits and vegetables, from apples to zucchini.

In addition to salsas, several types of ethnic sauces are often found in restaurant-style wraps. Chinese hoisin sauce, Japanese teriyaki sauce, southwestern barbecue sauce, Thai peanut sauce and Indian curry sauce and chutney are just some of the interesting choices offered.

Despite the mouth-watering variety of prepared salsas and sauces on the market, many home cooks enjoy making their own salsas and sauces from fresh ingredients. Following are several tempting choices for adding sparkle to your homemade wraps.

SALSA FRESCA

Makes about 2 cups

Popular salsa fresca can also be called red salsa. It is a common addition to Mexican-style wraps. Leave the salsa chunky and it becomes "Pico de Gallo." Adjust the amount of chile peppers to yield mild, medium or hot salsa.

4 medium plum tomatoes, cored, seeded and diced
½ cup finely chopped red onion
2 tbs. finely chopped red bell pepper
2–3 fresh serrano or other chile peppers, seeded and finely chopped

1 tbs. finely chopped fresh cilantro
1 tsp. fresh lime juice
salt and freshly ground pepper to taste

With a blender or food processor, blend all ingredients until almost smooth, but still with some texture. Transfer salsa to a glass bowl, cover and let stand for at least 30 minutes to blend flavors. Store tightly covered in the refrigerator for up to 1 week.

VARIATION: PICO DE GALLO

In a glass bowl, mix ingredients together. Let stand for about 30 minutes to blend flavors.

MANGO-PEAR SALSA

Inspired by Thai cuisine, this salsa is delicious with meat and chicken wraps. When fresh mangos are out of season, look for them frozen, in jars or in cans.

2 mangos, peeled and cut into ¼-inch cubes (about 1 cup)
2 ripe pears, peeled and cut into ¼-inch cubes
¼ cup freshly squeezed lime juice
1 serrano or jalapeño chile pepper, seeded and minced

3 green onions, finely sliced
⅔ cup coarsely chopped fresh cilantro, lightly packed
¼ red bell pepper, seeded, ribs removed and diced
salt and pepper to taste

With a blender or food processor, blend all ingredients until almost smooth, but still with some texture. Transfer mixture to a glass bowl, cover and let stand for at least 30 minutes to blend flavors. Store tightly covered in the refrigerator for up to 1 week.

VARIATION: CHUNKY MANGO SALSA

Increase mangos to 4 and omit pear. Mix all ingredients together in a glass bowl. Cover and let stand for at least 30 minutes to blend flavors.

PAPAYA SALSA

The best time to make this is when Mexican papayas are in season. Double or triple the recipe when serving a crowd.

1 large papaya, peeled, seeded and diced
¼ cup diced red bell pepper
¼ cup diced green onions
1 clove garlic, minced
2 serrano chile peppers, seeded and minced
¼ cup fresh lime juice
¼ cup pineapple juice
3 tbs. olive oil
3 tbs. chopped fresh cilantro
salt and freshly ground pepper to taste

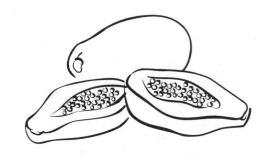

In a glass bowl, mix all ingredients well. Cover and refrigerate for 30 minutes to blend flavors. Store tightly covered in the refrigerator for up to 1 week.

PINEAPPLE SALSA

This salsa has a tangy, sweet-sour flavor with just enough bite to enhance meat and vegetable wraps. Tomatillos are small tomato-like fruits common in Latin American cooking. They are available in Latin American markets and some supermarkets. Before using tomatillos, remove the brown papery husk that surrounds them and wash well.

1 cup crushed pineapple with juice
4 tomatillos, finely chopped
¼ cup chopped red bell pepper
¼ cup chopped green bell pepper
1 tbs. cider vinegar
1 tbs. brown sugar
2 tsp. chopped fresh cilantro
salt and pepper to taste

With a blender or food processor, blend ingredients until almost smooth, but still with some texture. Transfer mixture to a glass bowl, cover and let stand for at least 30 minutes to blend flavors. Store tightly covered in the refrigerator for up to 1 week.

CUCUMBER SALSA

Since these ingredients are available year-round, cucumber salsa can always be handy in the refrigerator. Cucumber balances sweet or hot tastes.

3 ripe tomatoes, seeded and chopped
1 cucumber, peeled, seeded and chopped
½ medium-sized sweet red onion, chopped
2 tbs. chopped fresh basil
2 tbs. olive oil
2 tbs. red wine vinegar
½ tsp. Dijon-style mustard
¼ tsp. sugar
¼ tsp. salt
⅛ tsp. pepper

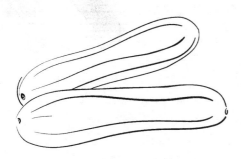

With a blender or food processor, blend ingredients until almost smooth, but still with some texture. Transfer mixture to a glass bowl, cover and let stand for at least 30 minutes to blend flavors. Store tightly covered in the refrigerator for up to 1 week.

TOMATILLO-APPLE SALSA

Tomatillos are small, tart green fruits that resemble tomatoes. In season, tomatillos are available where fresh chile peppers are sold; or, look for them in cans. If using fresh, remove the tomatillos' papery brown husk and wash them well before using. Try this recipe with or without the apple or with other fruits such as pear or mango. It is excellent with seafood.

4 tomatillos, halved or quartered
¼ cup pineapple juice
¼ cup orange juice
¼ cup fresh lime juice (from about 2 limes)
¼ cup white vinegar
4 tsp. minced garlic
1 tsp. red pepper flakes

¼ cup chopped fresh cilantro
1 red onion, finely chopped
1 red bell pepper, seeded, ribs removed and finely chopped
3 medium-sized red or green apples, peeled and coarsely chopped

In a blender container, combine tomatillos, pineapple juice, orange juice, lime juice, vinegar, garlic, pepper flakes and cilantro; blend until pureed. Place onion, bell pepper and apples in a glass bowl, add pureed mixture and mix well. Cover and refrigerate for about 2 hours to blend flavors. Store tightly covered in the refrigerator for up to 1 week.

MILD GUACAMOLE

Makes about 1 1/2 cups

Although mild, this guacamole has enough bite to make it interesting. Avocado lends color, flavor and texture to a wrap or roll-up. For a chunky guacamole, dice 1/2 avocado and mix it with the mashed avocado.

2 large, ripe Hass avocados, peeled and
   chopped
1 tbs. Dijon-style mustard
1/4 cup chili sauce
1 tbs. fresh lemon or lime juice
1 tbs. chopped red or green bell pepper,
   optional
1 tsp. Tabasco Sauce
salt and pepper to taste

In a bowl or with a food processor, mash avocados. Stir in remaining ingredients. Store tightly covered in the refrigerator for up to 1 day.

SPICY HOT GUACAMOLE

Makes about 1½ cups

Guacamole has as many variations as there are people who love it. Adjust the flavorings to taste. For a chunky version, dice ½ avocado and mix it with the mashed avocado.

2 large, ripe Hass avocados, peeled and chopped
2 tbs. chopped canned green chiles
1 clove garlic, minced
2 tbs. minced fresh cilantro
2 tbs. chopped green onions
1–2 tsp. ground cumin
2 tbs. fresh lemon or lime juice
dash Tabasco Sauce
¼–1 red jalapeño chile pepper, seeded and minced

In a bowl or with a food processor, mash avocados. Stir in remaining ingredients. Store tightly covered in the refrigerator for up to 1 day.

PEANUT-BARBECUE SAUCE

Makes about 1½–2 cups

Peanut sauce, a staple of Thai cuisine, is delicious combined with chicken and meat dishes. Look for chipotle (smoked jalapeño) packed in sauce in the Mexican food aisle of your supermarket or in specialty food stores. The can or jar may be labeled "Chipotles in Adobo." Chipotles have a wonderful, smoky taste. However, beware of their spicy kick.

½ cup smooth or crunchy peanut butter
½ cup purchased barbecue sauce
3 tbs. soy sauce
2–3 tbs. minced chipotle chiles in sauce

With a food processor or blender, mix all ingredients until well blended. Store tightly covered in the refrigerator for up to 3 days.

PEANUT-COCONUT SAUCE

This variation of Thai peanut sauce adds a pleasantly sweet flavor to meats and chicken in wraps. Use it as a sauce, or to dress crunchy vegetables or greens. Fish sauce (nam pla) is made from fermented salted fish. It resembles soy sauce in texture and color, but has a wonderful, unique flavor. Look for it in the international food section of the supermarket or in Asian markets.

½ cup creamy peanut butter
1 cup coconut milk
1 tbs. brown sugar
1 tsp. finely chopped fresh cilantro
¼ tsp. red pepper flakes
2 tsp. Thai fish sauce (nam pla)
1 tbs. rice or cider vinegar

With a food processor or blender, mix all ingredients until well blended. Store tightly covered in the refrigerator for up to 3 days.

PEANUT-CURRY-GINGER SAUCE

Sweet and spicy flavors blend to add a distinctive taste to wraps of almost any type. Try it with Indian and Middle Eastern ingredients.

1 cup low-fat mayonnaise
3 tbs. curry powder
1½ tbs. white wine vinegar
2 tbs. grated fresh lemon peel (zest)
2½ tsp. paprika
¼ cup chunky peanut butter
1 tsp. minced fresh ginger
½ tsp. salt
½ tsp. cayenne pepper

With a food processor or blender, mix all ingredients until well blended. Store tightly covered in the refrigerator for up to 1 week.

SESAME-GINGER-ORANGE SAUCE

Makes about 3/4 cup

The sweet and tangy flavor of this combination adds another dimension to a vegetarian wrap.

½ tsp. grated fresh orange peel (zest)
½ cup orange juice
3 tbs. soy sauce
1 clove garlic, minced
2 tsp. honey
1 tsp. minced fresh ginger
1 tsp. Asian sesame oil
1 tbs. sesame seeds

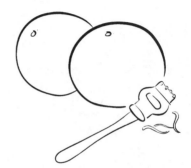

In a bowl, mix all ingredients together. Store tightly covered in the refrigerator for up to 3 days.

TAHINI SAUCE

Tahini, or sesame seed paste, can be found in the deli or health food sections of the super-market. It may also be available in jars in the international foods section or near the peanut butter. This sauce can be made mild or spicy by the addition of chili powder or chile peppers to taste. It goes well with everything: vegetables, meat, poultry and fish.

1 tbs. tahini
juice of 1 lemon
2 medium cloves garlic, minced
2 tsp. minced fresh ginger
½ tbs. soy sauce

½ tbs. sesame or peanut oil, optional
2 tbs. water
salt and pepper to taste
chili powder to taste

Combine all ingredients in a jar with a lid and shake vigorously for about 30 seconds, until well mixed. Store in refrigerator and shake well before using. Store tightly covered in the refrigerator for up to 2 days.

CUCUMBER-YOGURT SAUCE

This wonderful sauce tastes delicious with Middle Eastern lamb and beef wraps. It's good with vegetables, too.

1 medium cucumber, peeled, seeded and finely chopped
8 oz. low-fat plain yogurt
2 tsp. white wine vinegar
1 tbs. chopped fresh dill or mint
1 clove garlic, minced
salt and pepper to taste

Place cucumber in a colander to drain for a few minutes. Transfer cucumber to a bowl and mix with remaining ingredients. Store tightly covered in the refrigerator for up to 2 days.

APPLE CHUTNEY

Chutneys can be refrigerated for up to 3 weeks, or stored longer if placed in sterilized canning jars while hot.

6 large Fuji, Rome Beauty or Granny Smith apples, peeled and diced
½ cup finely chopped green bell pepper
½ cup minced onion
grated peel (zest) of 1/2 small lemon
1 cup white vinegar

¼ cup grainy mustard
1 cup raisins
½ cup brown sugar, firmly packed
½ tsp. ground cloves
½ tsp. ground nutmeg
½ tsp. ground allspice

In a 3-quart saucepan, combine all ingredients and bring to a boil, stirring often. Reduce heat to low, cover and simmer for 1 to 2 hours, stirring frequently, until chutney is dark and syrupy and apples are very soft. Cool and refrigerate. Store tightly covered in the refrigerator for up to 1 week.

PEAR OR PEACH CHUTNEY: Substitute 5 cups sliced peeled pears or peaches for apples.

PLUM CHUTNEY: Substitute 6 cups sliced peeled blue plums for apples.

MANGO CHUTNEY: Substitute 5 cups diced peeled mangos for apples.

WRAPS AND ROLL-UPS
WITH VEGETARIAN FILLINGS

A GARDEN OF OPTIONS

The vegetarian wrap is giving a distinctly American twist to the Mexican burrito. These nutritious, low-fat combinations will appeal to the cravings of a health-conscious audience.

With wraps, the key is in the assembly. In addition to the recipes that follow, use what you have on hand to create wonderful vegetarian wraps: use leftovers, raid the vegetable bin or root around in the garden; pick your favorite accompaniments and wrap them all in a colorful tortilla.

- Combine cooked potatoes and grilled vegetables with *Peanut-Curry Ginger Sauce,* page 57, and torn romaine lettuce.

- Combine jicama, peas, alfalfa sprouts, cucumbers and cole slaw with *Creamy Vinaigrette,* page 41. Wrap in a spinach or plain tortilla.

- Combine Spanish rice with grilled mixed vegetables, purple onions, goat cheese and *Salsa Fresca,* page 47. Wrap in a tomato tortilla.

- Combine diced firm tofu, cucumbers, red peppers, feta cheese, black olives, red onion, Spanish rice and *Chunky Mango Salsa,* page 48. Wrap in a spinach tortilla.

FARMER'S GARDEN WRAPS

Wholesome ingredients stuffed into a large tortilla make an ample, healthy lunch or dinner.

½ tsp. butter
1 cup sliced white mushrooms
1 cup thinly sliced green bell peppers
3 ripe salad tomatoes, diced
1 cup fresh or canned corn kernels
2 cups torn red leaf lettuce, small pieces

½ cup low-fat sour cream
½ cup roasted sunflower kernels
3 tbs. crumbled goat cheese
2 cups cooked jasmine rice, see Basic Rice, page 29
8 large whole wheat tortillas

In a large skillet, melt butter over medium heat and sauté mushrooms, peppers, tomatoes and corn until slightly soft. Transfer mixture to a large bowl with lettuce, sour cream, sunflower kernels and goat cheese. Add rice and mix ingredients well. Lay tortillas on a work surface and divide filling mixture among tortillas. Wrap according to desired style on pages 4 to 6. Serve slightly warm or cold.

ROASTED VEGETABLE MEDLEY WRAPS

Makes 6

Roasting, instead of sautéing, vegetables gives them a wonderful, succulent quality. Peanuts add crunch and flavor.

¼ cup diced zucchini
¼ cup diced yellow crookneck squash
¼ diced yellow bell pepper
¼ cup diced broccoli
¼ cup diced red onion
1 tbs. vegetable oil
1 tbs. balsamic vinegar

salt and pepper to taste
¼ cup shelled, roasted, unsalted peanuts
1 cup *Salsa Fresca*, page 47
8 large whole wheat tortillas, warmed
2 cups hot cooked jasmine rice (see *Basic Rice*, page 29)
¼ cup warmed canned pinto beans

Heat oven to 300°. In a large bowl, toss zucchini, yellow squash, bell pepper, broccoli, onion, oil, vinegar, salt and pepper. Transfer to a large baking sheet and roast for 15 minutes, turning once or twice with a spatula. Add peanuts to pan and roast for 5 minutes. Stir in salsa, taste and adjust seasonings. Lay tortillas on a work surface and layer with rice, beans and vegetable mixture. Wrap according to desired style on pages 4 to 6. Serve warm.

HAWAIIAN-STYLE FRUIT AND COCONUT WRAPS

Makes 6–8

Team brown rice with fresh apples, dried fruits, coconut and a dollop of sour cream for a deliciously different hot main course. Or, serve the filling cold as a dessert wrapped in a fruit-flavored tortilla.

1 cup uncooked brown rice
2½ cups water
1 medium apple, diced
¼ cup pitted prunes, quartered
¼ cup dried apricots

½ cup raisins
½ cup shredded coconut
6 medium flour tortillas, warmed
½ cup low-fat sour cream, optional

In a medium saucepan, combine rice and water and bring to a boil. Stir in apple, prunes, apricots and raisins; reduce heat to very low and cook, covered, for about 45 minutes, until all water is absorbed. Remove pan from heat, uncover pan, fluff rice with a fork and stir in fruit. Let mixture stand for 5 minutes. Stir in coconut. Lay tortillas on a work surface and divide filling mixture among tortillas. Top each with a dollop of sour cream, if using. Wrap according to desired style on pages 4 to 6.

WILD RICE WRAPS WITH CHILES AND GOAT CHEESE   Makes 8

Soft white goat cheese adds a unique flavor to this colorful, easy-to-make wrap. Look for canned "Chipotles in Adobo Sauce" in the Mexican food aisle of the supermarket or in Latin American markets.

¾ cup uncooked wild rice
1 pkg. (10 oz.) frozen whole kernel corn, thawed
1 sweet red bell pepper, seeded, ribs removed and diced
1 medium-sized red onion, diced
2 canned chipotle chile peppers with 2 tsp. sauce minced
½ cup chopped celery

about 1½ cups *Spicy Black Beans*, page 36, or 1 can (8 oz.) black beans, drained
½ cup coarsely shredded romaine or leaf lettuce
½ cup chopped fresh cilantro
½ cup crumbled goat cheese
1 tbs. olive oil
8 large spinach tortillas

Cook rice according to instructions on page 29 or on package. Five minutes before the end of cooking time, add corn and red pepper. Transfer mixture to a large bowl and add onion, chipotle chile peppers and sauce, celery, black beans, lettuce, cilantro, goat cheese and olive oil and toss together lightly. Lay tortillas on a work surface and divide filling mixture among tortillas. Wrap according to desired style on pages 4 to 6.

HALE, HEARTY, HEALTHY WRAPS

For this pretty wrap, steam an assortment of vegetables until slightly soft. It's a good idea to cook the vegetables separately, as each will take a slightly different length of time to cook.

1 cup small broccoli florets
1 cup small cauliflower florets
½ cup 1-inch-long asparagus pieces
½ cup diced yellow summer squash
1 cup drained, quartered, marinated
   artichoke hearts
2 cups shredded lettuce
1 tbs. safflower or olive oil

2 tbs. cider vinegar or white wine vinegar
¼ tsp. salt
⅛ tsp. pepper
10 medium flour, or other flavored tortillas
mustard or tomato salsa for spreading
2 cups *Mild Guacamole,* page 58, or
   mashed avocado
½ cup alfalfa or other sprouts

Separately, steam or microwave broccoli, cauliflower, asparagus and squash until tender-crisp; drain. Place steamed vegetables in a bowl and add artichoke hearts, shredded lettuce, oil, vinegar, salt and pepper. Toss until well mixed.

Lay tortillas on a work surface. Spread a strip of mustard or salsa along the center of each tortilla. Layer with steamed vegetables, guacamole and sprouts. Wrap according to desired style on pages 4 to 6.

SWEET-SOUR VEGETABLE WRAPS

This colorful wrap with a tangy sauce can be made ahead of time.

¼ cup rice vinegar or white wine vinegar
1 small Granny Smith apple, grated
½ tbs. sugar
½ tbs soy sauce
¼ tsp. salt
¼ tsp. Tabasco Sauce
1 tbs. sesame oil
2 cups shredded red cabbage
2 cups shredded green cabbage
½ cup shredded carrots

½ cup roasted sunflower kernels
¼ cup each thinly sliced red onion
¼ cup thinly sliced red bell pepper
¼ cup thinly sliced green bell pepper
1 can (4 oz.) sliced black olives, drained
¼ cup thinly sliced green onions
8–10 medium flour or spinach tortillas
½ cup *Chunky Mango Salsa,* page 48, or
   Apple Chutney, page 66
¾ cup alfalfa or other sprouts

In a large bowl, combine vinegar, apple, sugar, soy sauce, salt and Tabasco. Mix well with a wire whisk. Slowly add sesame oil and mix until ingredients are well blended. Add cabbages, carrots, sunflower kernels, onion, peppers, olives and green onions and toss well. Cover bowl and refrigerate for 1 hour to blend flavors, stirring occasionally. Drain before using. Lay tortillas on a work surface. Divide filling mixture evenly among tortillas and top with salsa and sprouts. Wrap according to desired style on pages 4 to 6.

MOROCCAN WRAPS WITH COUSCOUS AND DRIED FRUIT

For this North African-style wrap, substitute any dried fruits that are available and, perhaps, sweet potatoes for red potatoes.

¼ cup olive oil
1 medium-sized yellow onion, minced
1 clove garlic, minced
1 tbs. fresh ginger, minced
½ tsp. cinnamon
¼ tsp. cayenne pepper
¼ tsp. paprika
2 large carrots, peeled and cut into ¼-inch cubes
2 medium-sized red potatoes, peeled and cut into ¼-inch cubes

1 red bell pepper, seeded, ribs removed and diced
5 cups chicken stock
½ cup raisins
½ cup quartered dried prunes
½ cup quartered dried apricots
2 cups instant couscous
10–12 large flour or wheat tortillas, warmed
2 ripe tomatoes, diced
½ cup chopped fresh cilantro
10–12 leaves lettuce

In a large skillet, heat olive oil over medium heat and sauté onion until transparent. Add garlic, ginger, cinnamon, pepper and paprika and sauté for 30 seconds. Add carrots, potatoes and red bell pepper and sauté for 5 minutes, or until vegetables turn slightly brown. Stir in chicken stock and bring to boil over high heat. Reduce heat to low and add raisins, prunes and apricots. Cover skillet and simmer for 10 minutes, or until vegetables are tender. Stir in couscous, cover and remove from heat. Let stand for 3 to 5 minutes, until couscous is soft and fluffy and liquid has been absorbed.

Lay tortillas on a work surface. Divide filling mixture evenly among tortillas and top with tomatoes, cilantro and lettuce leaves. Wrap according to desired style on pages 4 to 6.

POTATOES, BEANS AND GOOD STUFF WRAPS

Makes 6

Potatoes combined with crisp red and green bell peppers provide texture and color for a tasty, eye-appealing wrap. If desired, you can substitute guacamole for the sour cream.

1 tbs. vegetable oil
1 red onion, thinly sliced
1 tsp. dried thyme
1 tsp. dried marjoram
4 medium-sized white or red potatoes, cooked until just firm, peeled and diced
1 cup drained cooked *Mexican-Style Pinto Beans*, made without ham, page 37, or use
   canned
1 can (8 oz.) sweet corn, drained
1 medium-sized green bell pepper, seeded, ribs removed and thinly sliced
1 medium-sized red bell pepper, seeded, ribs removed and thinly sliced
6 large flour tortillas, warmed
½ cup *Salsa Fresca*, page 47
½ cup sour cream or plain yogurt

In a large skillet, heat vegetable oil over medium heat and sauté onion, thyme and marjoram for about 2 minutes, or until onion is softened. Add diced potatoes and cook for about 10 minutes, tossing occasionally, until potatoes are lightly browned. Add pinto beans and corn and cook for about 5 minutes, until heated through. Add red and green peppers and cook until warm, but still crunchy, about 1 minute.

Lay tortillas on a work surface. Divide potato mixture evenly among tortillas and top with salsa and sour cream. Wrap according to desired style on pages 4 to 6.

ZUCCHINI, JICAMA AND TWO-BEAN WRAPS

For this wrap, crisp colorful vegetables provide contrast to soft beans. Use different cheeses and salsas for variety.

4 medium zucchini
2 tsp. vegetable oil
¼ chopped red onion
¼ tsp. ground cinnamon
2 tbs. dried cilantro
1 can (15 oz.) Spanish-style red kidney beans, drained
1 can (15–19 oz.) low-fat refried beans
2 cups torn fresh spinach leaves

2 medium-sized red bell peppers, seeded, ribs removed and cut into bite-sized pieces
1 cup bite-sized jicama pieces
6 large flour tortillas
1 cup shredded Monterey Jack cheese
¼ cup fresh cilantro leaves, loosely packed
1¼ cups *Tomatillo-Apple Salsa*, page 52, or *Spicy Hot Guacamole*, page 54, optional

Cut zucchini lengthwise into quarters and cut quarters crosswise into slices. In a large non-stick skillet or wok, heat oil over medium-high heat and sauté onion and zucchini for 3 to 5 minutes, until softened. Stir in cinnamon and cilantro. Reduce heat to low, add kidney beans and refried beans and cook, stirring occasionally, until heated through. Stir in spinach and cook for 1 minute. Stir in red peppers and jicama.

Lay tortillas on a work surface. Place about 1 cup of the filling on each tortilla and sprinkle with cheese and cilantro. Top with salsa or guacamole, or a combination of the two. Wrap according to desired style on pages 4 to 6.

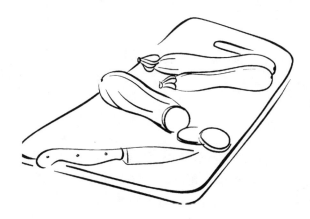

BLACK BEAN, CORN AND TOMATO WRAPS

Vary this combination with other flavorings, such as sun-dried tomatoes, fresh chives, fresh basil or curry powder. Intensify the "heat" with hot chiles and salsa.

1 can (15–19 oz.) black beans, rinsed and drained
1 can (15–16 oz.) whole-kernel corn, drained
1 can (4 oz.) chopped mild green chiles, drained
2/3 cup shredded Monterey Jack or cheddar cheese
1/4 cup chopped fresh cilantro
2 cups cooked jasmine rice (see *Basic Rice*, page 29)
8 large flour tortillas
1 cup *Cucumber Salsa*, page 51, or other mild salsa
1 cup coarsely chopped tomatoes

In a large bowl, combine black beans, corn, chiles, cheese and cilantro and mix well. Stir in cooked rice. Lay tortillas on a work surface and place about 1 cup of the filling on each tortilla. Top with salsa and chopped tomatoes, dividing evenly. Wrap according to desired style on pages 4 to 6.

HOT-HOT TOMATO-BEAN WRAPS

Season this to your liking by adjusting the amount of chiles. Serve extra sauce and chopped onions on the side.

1 can (15-19 oz.) black beans, rinsed and drained
4 small ripe tomatoes, diced
4 cloves garlic, minced
1 onion, finely chopped
1 Anaheim chile, seeded, ribs removed and chopped, or 1 can (4oz.) chopped green chiles
½ tsp. dried thyme

½ tsp. dried oregano
½ tsp. dried cilantro
ground cumin to taste
½ cup *Salsa Fresca*, page 47, or *Spicy Hot Guacamole*, Page 54
6 large flour tortillas
1 cup shredded lettuce

In a large bowl, combine beans, tomatoes, garlic, onion, chile, thyme, oregano, cilantro, cumin and salsa and mix well. Lay tortillas on a work surface and divide filling evenly among tortillas. Top filling with lettuce and wrap according to desired style on pages 4 to 6.

TERIYAKI TOFU WRAPS

Lightly browned tofu adds flavor, nutrition and texture to a vegetarian wrap. Pineapple is a nice complement to teriyaki flavors.

1 tbs. vegetable oil
1 white onion, chopped
1½ cups firm tofu, cut into ½-inch squares
1 cup broccoli florets
1 cup sliced white mushrooms
1 can (20 oz.) pineapple chunks, drained

½ cup teriyaki sauce
1 cup cooked jasmine rice (see *Basic Rice*, page 29)
4–5 large flour or flavored tortillas
¼ cup *Pineapple Salsa*, page 50

In a medium skillet or wok, heat vegetable oil over medium heat. Add onion and tofu and sauté until tofu is browned. Add broccoli florets and mushrooms and sauté until soft, about 3 minutes. Stir in pineapple and teriyaki sauce. Stir in prepared rice. Lay tortillas on a work surface and divide filling evenly among tortillas. Top filling with salsa and wrap according to desired style on pages 4 to 6.

SWEET POTATO AND EGG WRAPS

Here's a perfect combination for breakfast or brunch. Bake the sweet potatoes ahead of time and refrigerate; this makes them easy to cube.

3 medium-sized sweet potatoes, baked until tender, but still slightly firm, and peeled
1 tbs. butter
1 red bell pepper, seeded, ribs removed and diced
8 large eggs, lightly beaten
salt and pepper to taste
8 flour or spinach tortillas, warmed
½ cup *Pineapple Salsa*, page 50, plus more if desired

Slice sweet potatoes into ½-inch rounds and cut each round into quarters. In a large skillet, heat butter over medium heat. Add potatoes and sauté for about 2 minutes. Stir in bell pepper. Pour eggs over potatoes and peppers and scramble gently, seasoning with salt and pepper. Cook until eggs are set and remove from heat. Lay tortillas on a work surface and divide filling evenly among tortillas. Top with salsa and fold each tortilla in half. Serve wraps on a plate with extra salsa on the side, if desired.

FALAFEL-TAHINI WRAPS

Speed up the preparation for this tasty Middle Eastern delicacy by using a prepared falafel mix. This is especially good on pita or lavosh. Instead of tahini sauce, you can use prepared sesame, cucumber or other salad dressing. Change the flavor of the garnishes infinitely by adding other vegetables, such as bell peppers, black olives or pickled turnips or beets.

1 pkg. (6 oz.) falafel mix
4 lavosh, pita breads or large flour tortillas, warmed
8 leaves romaine lettuce, coarsely shredded
2 medium-sized ripe tomatoes, chopped
2 tbs. chopped red onion
½ cup coarsely chopped pimiento-stuffed green olives
¼ cup *Tahini Sauce*, page 59, or other salad dressing

Prepare falafel mix according to package directions and form into 12 patties about 2-inches in diameter and ½-inch thick. Cook falafel according to package directions and keep warm. Lay lavosh on a work surface and place ¼ of the lettuce leaves on each lavosh. In a bowl, mix tomatoes, onion and olives and spoon over lettuce; drizzle with *Tahini Sauce*. Place 3 of the falafel patties on each wrap. Fold wrap, cut in half and serve.

SPINACH, TOFU AND MUSHROOM ROLL-UPS Makes about 40 pieces

Use this platter as a buffet centerpiece. Line a tray with arugula or colorful Bibb lettuce.

1 red onion, thinly sliced
1 tbs. vegetable oil
1 lb. firm tofu, cut into small pieces
1 cup sliced white mushrooms
2 pkg. (10 oz. each) frozen spinach, thawed
   and squeezed dry

1 cup low-fat mayonnaise
1 pkg. (1 oz.) dry herb soup/dip mix
½ cup plain yogurt or low-fat sour cream
8 large flour tortillas, or 4 lavosh
1 cup bite-sized pieces leafy lettuce, or 2
   cups shredded green cabbage

Mince enough of the sliced onion to equal ¼ cup. In a medium skillet, heat oil over medium heat and sauté ¼ cup minced onion with tofu until tofu is brown. Add mushrooms and sauté for 2 minutes; cool. In a large bowl, mix together spinach, mayonnaise, soup mix and all but 1 tbs. of the yogurt. Add cooled tofu mixture and mix well. Place tortillas on a work surface and spread tofu mixture over each tortilla, leaving a ½-inch border. Arrange sliced red onion over the top, followed by lettuce pieces. Spread edges of tortilla lightly with remaining 1 tbs. yogurt. Wrap fillings roll-up-style (pages 4 to 6) into a log and wrap tightly with plastic wrap; twist ends to secure. Refrigerate log for 2 hours or overnight. Remove log from refrigerator, remove waxed paper and slice log into 1½-inch rounds.

MIDDLE EASTERN HUMMUS ROLL-UPS

Makes about 30 pieces

Hummus is a garbanzo bean dish with origins in Greece, Turkey and Lebanon. Here it is teamed with vegetables and feta cheese in a green spinach tortilla.

2 cans (15½ oz. each) garbanzo beans
¼-½ cup lemon juice
1 tbs. olive oil
3 cloves garlic, minced
½ cup chopped Italian parsley
½ tsp. salt
½ tsp. paprika
6 large flour or spinach tortillas
1 medium zucchini, cut lengthwise into thin slices
1 large cucumber, cut lengthwise into thin slices
1 jar (12 oz.) roasted red bell peppers, drained, patted dry and thinly sliced
½ cup drained sliced black olives
¼ lb. feta cheese, crumbled
6 large leaves lettuce, patted dry
2 tbs. plain yogurt or sour cream

Drain garbanzo beans, reserving bean liquid. With a food processor, puree garbanzo beans with lemon juice. Add reserved bean liquid, a little at a time, until puree is spreading consistency, but not soupy. Stir in oil, garlic, parsley, salt and paprika. Cover and refrigerate mixture for at least 1 hour to blend flavors; it will keep for several days.

Lay tortillas on a work surface and spread garbanzo bean mixture over each tortilla, dividing evenly and leaving a ½-inch border. Arrange zucchini, cucumber and peppers over hummus, dividing evenly. Sprinkle with olives and feta cheese and top with lettuce. Spread edges of tortilla lightly with yogurt. Wrap fillings roll-up-style (see pages 4 to 6) into a log and wrap tightly with plastic wrap; twist ends to secure. Refrigerate log for 2 hours or overnight. Remove log from refrigerator, remove waxed paper and slice log into 1½-inch rounds.

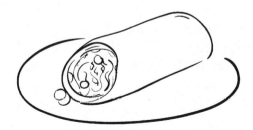

AVOCADO-CRANBERRY ROLL-UPS

Vegetarian, healthy and colorful, this wrap's a winner. The lettuce serves as a barrier so that the soft ingredients stay separate during rolling.

2 large tortillas, any flavor, or 2 lavosh
8 leaves romaine lettuce, tough ribs removed
¾ cup *Mild Guacamole*, page 53
½ cucumber, slivered
1 ripe tomato, quartered and sliced
2 tbs. crumbled feta cheese
¾ cup whole-berry cranberry sauce

Lay tortillas or lavosh on a work surface. Place 2 of the lettuce leaves at the center of each tortilla, or near the end of the lavosh. Spread guacamole over lettuce. Top guacamole with a layer of cucumber followed by layers of tomato and feta cheese. Place 2 lettuce leaves on top of feta cheese and gently spoon cranberry sauce on top of lettuce. Wrap fillings roll-up-style (see pages 4 to 6) into a log and wrap tightly with plastic wrap. Refrigerate for at least 1 hour before serving. Remove log from refrigerator, remove plastic and slice log into 1½-inch rounds.

84   VEGETARIAN FILLINGS

LETTUCE WRAPS

STIR-FRY PORK IN LETTUCE WRAPS

Makes 8–10

For those who like their food hot and spicy.

8–10 iceberg lettuce leaves
1 tbs.canola oil
2 cloves garlic, crushed, or 1 tsp. crushed
  garlic
2 tsp. grated ginger or 1 tsp. crushed ginger
2 chiles, diced and seeded, or 1 tsp. crushed
  red pepper flakes

2 lb. pork, minced
soy sauce to taste
4 green onions, chopped
chopped coriander or parsley to taste
chili sauce to taste
rice, optional

Peel whole leaves from a head of iceberg lettuce. Wash well, dry carefully with a paper towel and chill until needed. Heat a large, heavy frying pan or wok until hot. Add a drizzle of oil, garlic, ginger and chili and cook for 1 minute. Add pork and cook until browned. Add soy sauce, onions and coriander or parsley. Spoon ¼ of the mixture into each lettuce leaf, add a dollop of chili sauce and roll up. Serve immediately with steamed rice if desired.

BACON, SPINACH AND TOMATO LETTUCE WRAP

Putting all the ingredients into lettuce and creating a healthy low-calorie, low-carbohydrate wrap can replace triple-decker bread sandwiches.

12 slices bacon, fried crisp and crumbled
1 pkg. (8 oz.) vegetable-flavored cream cheese, cut into small pieces
2 tomatoes, seeded and chopped
1 avocado, thinly sliced
2 cups baby spinach leaves, chopped
alfalfa sprouts
8 iceberg lettuce leaves

Combine ingredients and chop into bite-sized morsels, divide into 8 servings and wrap in lettuce leaves.

TUSCANY CHICKEN AND TOMATOES IN LETTUCE LEAVES

Makes 8

When following a low-cholesterol, high-fiber, low-fat diet, here's a recipe that delivers what the doctor ordered.

2 chicken breast halves, cut into 1-inch cubes
salt and pepper for seasoning
1 small onion, coarsely chopped
6 mushrooms, sliced
1 medium tomato, seeded
½ green or red bell pepper
¼ tsp. dried thyme
8 iceberg lettuce leaves

Season chicken with salt and pepper. Over medium heat, brown chicken pieces in a little oil. Add remaining ingredients. Cover and simmer for 5 to 7 minutes. Drain any juices. Divide and serve in lettuce leaves.

TUNA IN A LETTUCE WRAP

With a can of tuna in the cupboard and a few vegetables, it's easy to whip up a meal. Substitute salmon if you prefer.

3½ oz. tuna in water
1 tbs. mayonnaise
½ tsp. lemon juice
¼ cup cooked, frozen or canned sweet corn, drained
1½ oz. cucumber, red pepper or celery, thinly sliced
4–6 large iceberg lettuce leaves
2 chives, optional

Drain tuna and mix with mayonnaise, lemon juice and paprika. Stir in sweet corn, cucumber and red pepper. Spoon tuna mix into each lettuce leaf, wrap and eat.

PORK AND SHRIMP LETTUCE WRAPS

Makes 4

This dish takes its cue from a traditional Thai lettuce parcel recipe. Satay sauce can be purchased ready-made from the ethnic food section of your supermarket.

1 oz. cellophane noodles, cooked
¼ cup mayonnaise
12 fresh mint leaves
8 oz. roast pork, cooked, and thinly sliced
4 jumbo shrimp cooked, shelled, cleaned, and quartered
satay sauce
4 butter or iceberg lettuce leaves

Cook noodles according to directions and let cool. Combine all other ingredients. Spoon noodles and other ingredients into lettuce leaves and add satay sauce to taste.

WRAPS AND ROLL-UPS
WITH BEEF, PORK AND LAMB

MEATY CHOICES

In any of the following recipes, you can substitute one kind of meat for another. Always drain fats from sautéed meats. Meat wraps can be reheated in an oven for 10 minutes at about 200°. Avoid overheating so that the raw vegetables, such as lettuce, don't become limp. Wraps can be heated briefly in the microwave if they are not wrapped in aluminum foil.

Use your imagination to make spur-of-the-moment meat wraps.

- Combine browned ground beef with black beans, lettuce, tomato, guacamole and cucumber with *Mango-Pear Salsa*, page 48. Wrap in a flour tortilla.

- Combine browned ground lamb with dried apricots, sunflower kernels, shredded cabbage and lime-flavored sour cream. Wrap in a flour tortilla.

- Combine grilled steak strips, mashed potatoes, corn kernels, black beans and *Classic Cole Slaw*, page 40, with *Peanut Barbecue Sauce*, page 55. Wrap in a sun-dried tomato tortilla.

- Combine marinated broiled skirt steak strips with mozzarella cheese, *Southwestern Rice*, page 31, sun-dried tomatoes, salsa and guacamole. Roll in a black bean tortilla.

ROAST BEEF AND RED CABBAGE WRAPS

Makes 4

Cut this wrap in half at a sharp angle. Arrange the halves so the cut sides show the colors within. Or wrap it roll-up style (see pages 4 to 6) and slice it for appetizers. Red horseradish is widely available; it gets it's color from beets.

1¼ cups shredded red cabbage
2 tsp. raspberry vinegar
2 tsp. vegetable oil
1 tsp. salt
1 tsp. freshly ground pepper

4 large flour or tomato tortillas
2 tbs. prepared horseradish
1 tbs. minced fresh dill, or 2 tsp. dried
1 cup large lettuce pieces
½ lb. roast beef, thinly sliced

In a medium bowl, toss cabbage with vinegar, oil, salt and pepper. Lay tortillas on a work surface. Spread a thin layer of horseradish on the center of each tortilla and sprinkle with a small amount of dill. Top with lettuce, roast beef, cabbage mixture and any remaining dill. Wrap according to desired style on pages 4 to 6.

SIRLOIN WRAPS WITH VEGETABLES AND BEANS

Makes 4

Broiled or barbecued steak adds great flavor to a wrap. Use charcoal made from hickory wood for an interesting smoky flavor and aroma.

1 can (16 oz.) fat-free, refried beans
1 tbs. olive or vegetable oil
1 red onion, thinly sliced
1 red bell pepper, thinly sliced
2 jalapeño chile peppers, seeded and minced
2 cloves garlic, minced
1 ripe tomato, diced

1½ lb. sirloin steak, fat trimmed, cut into ¼-inch thick strips, cut into bite-sized pieces
1 tbs. fresh lemon or lime juice
2 tbs. chopped fresh cilantro, or 2 tsp. dried
1 tsp. ground cumin
4 large flour tortillas, warmed
Papaya Salsa, page 54, or other salsa

Heat beans in a microwave oven or saucepan until heated through; keep warm. In a wok or heavy skillet, heat oil over medium-high heat and sauté onion for about 3 minutes, until almost translucent. Add bell pepper, jalapeño, garlic and tomato and sauté until heated through. Push mixture to one side of the pan. Add steak and stir-fry until no longer pink. Drain off any fat. Remove pan from heat and stir in lemon juice, cilantro and cumin.

Lay tortillas on a work surface. Divide beans among tortillas and top with steak-vegetable mixture. Top meat with salsa. Wrap according to desired style on pages 4 to 6.

SPEEDY BEEF AND VEGETABLE WRAPS

Serve these folded on a dish or wrapped in aluminum foil for eating on the run. Try the Corn Tortillas, page 24, as an alternative wrapper. They're not as flexible as flour tortillas, but their flavor goes nicely with the fillings.

1½ lb. ground beef
1 clove garlic, minced
2 tsp. chili powder
¼ tsp. ground cumin
1 tsp. dried cilantro
½ tsp. salt
¼ tsp. pepper
1¼ cups *Salsa Fresca,* page 47

2 pkg. (10 oz. each) frozen chopped
    spinach, thawed and well drained
1 cup frozen corn, thawed, or canned corn,
    drained
1 cup mixed shredded Monterey Jack,
    mozzarella and/or cheddar cheese
8 large flour tortillas, warmed

In a large nonstick skillet, sauté ground beef over medium heat for 10 to 12 minutes, until all traces of pink are gone from meat. Pour off drippings. Season beef with garlic, chili powder, cumin, cilantro, salt and pepper. Stir in salsa, spinach and corn and cook until heated through. Remove skillet from heat and stir in cheese. Lay tortillas on a work surface and divide filling mixture among tortillas. Wrap according to desired style on pages 4 to 6. Serve warm.

GARLIC STEAK WRAPS
WITH MINT YOGURT SAUCE

Feel free to substitute your favorite vegetables or herbs for the ones listed here.

3 cloves garlic, minced or pressed
3 tbs. soy sauce
1½ tsp. sugar
1 tbs. chopped fresh basil, or 2 tsp. dried
1 lb. lean boneless top sirloin, cut across the grain into ⅛-x-2-inch strips
1 tsp. vegetable oil
½ cup diced, cooked potato
3 green onions, cut into 1-inch slivers
½ cup slivered red bell pepper
1 cup nonfat plain yogurt
1 tbs. chopped fresh mint
1 tbs. chopped fresh cilantro
salt to taste
8 large flour tortillas
1 cup torn arugula leaves

In a large bowl, mix garlic, soy sauce, sugar and basil. Add steak strips to bowl, toss to coat well and let stand for 15 minutes, stirring occasionally.

In a wok or large nonstick skillet, heat oil over medium-high heat. Lift meat from marinade and stir-fry until desired doneness. Transfer steak to a covered dish to keep warm. In wok, stir-fry potato, green onion and pepper for about 3 minutes, until soft. In a bowl, stir together yogurt, mint, chopped cilantro and salt.

Lay tortillas on a work surface and divide vegetables and steak among tortillas. Top with arugula and a spoonful of mint-yogurt sauce. Wrap according to desired style on pages 4 to 6. Serve extra sauce on the side.

TURKISH-STYLE BEEF WRAPS

Makes 4

The star of this wrap is a Turkish-style cucumber salad. Here, it is combined with ground sirloin, but it can also garnish a vegetarian filling. Optionally, combine the salad with diced cooked lamb, chicken or turkey.

½ medium-sized red onion, thinly sliced
2 tbs. red wine vinegar
¼ tsp. kosher salt
1 large ripe tomato, diced
1 medium cucumber, peeled and diced
2 tsp. extra virgin olive oil

1 tbs. coarsely chopped fresh basil
salt and freshly ground pepper to taste
½ tsp. olive oil
½ lb. ground sirloin
4 large flour tortillas

In a medium bowl, toss red onion with vinegar and kosher salt and let stand for ten minutes; drain. Add tomato, cucumber, olive oil and basil and toss gently. Season with salt and pepper.

In a skillet, heat oil over medium-high heat and saute ground sirloin until no pink remains. Drain off fat and cool meat slightly. Transfer meat to bowl with cucumber mixture and toss well. Lay tortillas on a work surface and divide filling among tortillas. Wrap according to style on pages 4 to 6.

ARTICHOKE, CHEESE AND PROSCIUTTO WRAPS

Makes 2

This tasty combination makes gourmet wraps for any occasion. Cut it into smaller pieces for appetizers using the roll-up method, page 6.

4 oz. whipped cream cheese
1 tbs. finely chopped red onion
¼ cup drained, quartered marinated artichoke hearts
¼ cup sliced pimiento-stuffed green olives
1½ tbs. chopped fresh oregano, or 2 tsp. dried
2 tsp. dried rosemary
2 large flour tortillas
4 oz. Swiss or provolone cheese, thinly sliced
6 oz. prosciutto or ham, thinly sliced
6 large lettuce leaves, torn into pieces

In a medium bowl, stir together cream cheese, onion, artichoke hearts, olives, oregano and rosemary. Lay tortillas on a work surface and divide cream cheese mixture among tortillas. Top with Swiss cheese, prosciutto and lettuce. Wrap according to desired style on pages 4 to 6.

ITALIAN SAUSAGE WRAPS
WITH SPINACH AND CHEESE

Make these wraps in large batches and freeze. Or, make the filling and freeze it in individual portions in small plastic bags. Place the bag in the microwave or a pan of hot water to thaw and empty the contents onto a warmed tortilla. Asadero cheese is a soft white Mexican cheese, similar to mozzarella. It melts well without being rubbery. Look for it in stores with a specialty cheese section or in a Mexican market.

¼ cup olive oil
2–3 onions, thinly sliced
3–6 cloves garlic, minced
1 lb. white mushrooms, thinly sliced
3 lb. fresh spinach, well washed and dried, stems removed
2 lb. sweet or hot Italian sausage links, or a combination, casings removed

¼ cup minced fresh Italian parsley
1 cup ricotta cheese
2 cups grated Monterey Jack or asadero cheese ¼-½ cup freshly grated Parmesan cheese
salt and white pepper to taste
freshly grated nutmeg to taste
8 large flour tortillas, warmed

In a large skillet or wok, heat olive oil over medium heat and sauté onions and garlic for about 5 minutes, until golden. Add mushrooms and spinach and sauté over medium-high heat until spinach wilts.

In another skillet, break sausage into pieces with a fork and sauté until no pink remains. With a slotted spoon, transfer cooked sausage to paper towels to drain. Place drained cooked sausage in skillet with vegetables. Stir in parsley, ricotta and Monterey Jack cheese and season with salt, pepper and nutmeg.

Lay tortillas on a work surface and divide filling mixture among tortillas. Wrap according to desired style on pages 4 to 6.

NEW ORLEANS-STYLE CARNIVAL WRAPS

Red beans, rice and sausage are a mainstay of New Orleans cuisine. Ground beef can be substituted for sausage, if desired.

1 tbs. olive oil
12 oz. spicy smoked sausage, cut into 1-inch slices
1½ cups chopped onions
1 large green bell pepper, seeded, ribs removed and chopped
1 stalk celery, chopped
3 green onions, sliced
4 cups canned red beans, rinsed and drained
3 cups water
2 bay leaves
1 tsp. dried thyme
¼ tsp. freshly ground pepper
½ tsp. Tabasco Sauce
1 tsp. salt
1½ cups cooked long-grain rice (see *Basic Rice* page 29)
8–10 large flour, spinach or tomato tortillas

In a large, heavy stockpot, heat olive oil over medium heat. Add sausage and sauté for about 5 minutes, until it begins to brown. Drain fat and blot excess fat from meat with paper towels. To stockpot, add onion, bell pepper, celery and green onions and sauté for about 5 minutes, until vegetables begin to soften. Add beans, water, bay leaves, thyme and pepper and simmer over low heat for about 30 minutes.

With the back of a serving spoon, mash about ¼ of the beans against the side of the pot; stir well to thicken mixture. Season with Tabasco and salt. Add rice to bean mixture and mix well.

Lay tortillas on a work surface and divide filling among tortillas. Wrap according to desired style on pages 4 to 6.

CASBAH WRAPS

A combination of Moroccan-style lamb, rice pilaf and dried fruits is all made in one pot.

1 tbs. butter or vegetable oil
1½ lb. lamb stew meat, cut into 1-inch pieces
1 cup finely chopped onion
1 jalapeño chile, seeded and chopped
1 cup uncooked basmati or jasmine rice
1¾ cups chicken or vegetable stock
⅓ cup dry white wine
¼ tsp. saffron threads
½ cup quartered dried apricots
⅓ cup golden raisins
1 tsp. cinnamon
3 tbs. blanched slivered almonds, lightly toasted
1 tsp. finely grated fresh lemon peel (zest)
1 tbs. minced fresh chives, optional
8-10 large flour or jalapeño tortillas

In a heavy 4-quart saucepan, heat butter over medium-high heat. Dry lamb cubes with paper towels and add to pan; sauté for about 4 minutes, until almost brown. Add onion and jalapeño and sauté for about 3 minutes, until softened. Stir in rice and cook for 5 to 6 minutes, until rice is just beginning to turn brown. Stir in stock, wine, saffron, apricots, raisins and cinnamon and bring to a boil. Reduce heat to low, cover and simmer for about 12 to 14 minutes, until all liquid is absorbed. Remove pan from heat and uncover pan. Gently fluff rice with a fork and stir in almonds, lemon peel and chives, if using.

Lay tortillas on a work surface and divide lamb mixture among tortillas. Wrap according to desired style on pages 4 to 6.

LAMB AND PEPPER WRAPS

Toss the greens while the lamb is cooking and the tortillas are warming.

1 tbs. olive oil
1 lb. lean lamb, cut into thin strips
1 small onion, thinly sliced
1 each red and green bell peppers, seeded,
  ribs removed, thinly sliced
2 cloves garlic, minced
salt and pepper to taste
¼ cup extra virgin olive oil

2 tbs. balsamic vinegar
2 tsp. Dijon-style mustard
¼ tsp. salt
¼ tsp. pepper
4 cups torn salad greens
2 tbs. crumbled feta cheese
6 large flour tortillas

In large skillet, heat oil over medium-high heat and stir-fry lamb for 2 minutes. Add onions, peppers and garlic and stir-fry for 3 minutes, until lamb is cooked through and vegetables are softened, but still bright in color. Season with salt and pepper. In a glass measuring cup, combine extra virgin olive oil, vinegar, mustard, ¼ tsp. salt and ¼ tsp. pepper and mix well. Place salad greens in a large bowl and pour dressing over the top. Add feta cheese and toss well.

Lay tortillas on a work surface. Divide lamb mixture among tortillas and top with salad mixture. Wrap according to desired style on pages 4 to 6.

THAI-FLAVORED PORK WRAPS

Serve these on a plate with a side salad of leaf lettuce, cucumbers and thinly sliced red pepper.

1½ lb. lean ground pork
2 tbs. grated fresh ginger
1 clove garlic, minced
1 small onion, thinly sliced
2 cups chopped fresh broccoli or chopped
    fresh spinach
1 tbs. sesame oil
3 tbs. soy sauce

2 tbs. lime juice
1 tbs. honey
2 tsp. ground coriander
½ tsp. red pepper flakes
6 large flour tortillas, warmed
3 cups *Thai Slaw*, page 47
chopped fresh cilantro for garnish

In a large nonstick skillet over high heat, stir-fry pork for about 3 to 4 minutes, until no longer pink, crumbling into small pieces. Add ginger, garlic, onion and broccoli and stir-fry for 2 minutes. In a small bowl, mix sesame oil, soy sauce, lime juice, honey, coriander and pepper flakes and add to skillet. Stir-fry for about 1 minute, until mixture is well blended.

Lay tortillas on a work surface and divide pork mixture evenly among tortillas. Top with slaw and cilantro. Wrap according to desired style on pages 4 to 6.

CELEBRATION ROLL-UPS

It is easy to fashion roll-ups with different colors for holidays or special occasions.

CHRISTMAS ROLL-UPS

2 pkg. (16 oz. each) cream cheese, softened
1–2 drops red food coloring
1 medium-sized red bell pepper, seeded, ribs removed and finely minced
1 medium-sized green bell pepper, seeded, ribs removed and finely minced
1 pkg. (4 oz.) Ranch salad dressing mix
6 medium tomato tortillas
18 slices luncheon meat, such as roast beef, salami, prosciutto, mortadella or bologna
¼ cup sliced green onions
¼ cup sliced pimiento-stuffed green olives
2 Granny Smith apples, thinly sliced and brushed with lemon juice
2 Rome Beauty apples, thinly sliced and brushed with lemon juice
12 leaves bright, green lettuce

In a bowl, blend cream cheese with red food coloring. Add red and green peppers and dressing mix and blend until smooth and spreadable.

Lay tortillas on a work surface. Spread cream cheese mixture on tortillas, dividing evenly. Lay 3 bologna, overlapping slices, across the center of each tortilla. Sprinkle with onions and olives. Top with apples and lettuce leaves. Wrap fillings roll-up-style (see page 6) into a log and wrap tightly with plastic wrap; twist ends to secure. Refrigerate log for at least 2 hours or overnight. Remove log from refrigerator, remove plastic wrap and cut each log into 1- to 11/2-inch slices. Serve on a platter.

ST. PATRICK'S DAY ROLL-UPS: Mix cream cheese with dry herb salad dressing mix and spread over spinach tortillas. Layer thinly sliced corned beef, romaine lettuce leaves and diced green bell pepper over cream cheese and wrap roll-up style. Cut into slices to serve.

INDEPENDENCE DAY ROLL-UPS: Mix cream cheese with dried blueberries and spread over strawberry tortillas. Layer with sliced turkey, chopped red apples and chopped toasted walnuts and wrap roll-up style. Cut into slices to serve.

HALLOWEEN ROLL-UPS: Mix pureed cooked pumpkin or winter squash with rice and spread over black pepper and green chile tortillas. Layer with sliced ham and romaine lettuce and wrap roll-up style. Cut into slices to serve.

FRUITY ROLL-UPS WITH HAM

Makes 18–24 pieces

Serve these unique treats for breakfast, brunch or appetizers. If using lavosh, make sure to divide the fillings evenly among them.

1 pkg. (8 oz.) cream cheese, softened
1 can (8 oz.) crushed pineapple, well
    drained
¼ cup *Mango-Pear Salsa*, page 48, or other
    fruit salsa
¼ cup chopped walnuts or pecans
⅛ tsp. pumpkin pie spice

1 tsp. cinnamon
6 medium flour or tomato tortillas, or 4
    lavosh
18 thin slices ham
6–12 large leaves Bibb or romaine lettuce
    leaves, ribs removed

In a small bowl, mix cream cheese, pineapple, salsa, nuts, pumpkin pie spice and cinnamon. Lay tortillas on a work surface and spread with cream cheese mixture, dividing evenly. Lay 3 thin slices of ham, overlapping, across the center of tortilla. Top with 1 or 2 lettuce leaves. Wrap fillings roll-up-style (see page 6) into a log and wrap tightly with plastic wrap; twist ends to secure. Refrigerate log for at least 2 hours or overnight. Remove log from refrigerator, remove plastic wrap and cut each log into 3 to 4 pieces.

TURKEY AND ROAST BEEF ROLL-UPS

Makes 25–30 pieces

This favorite sandwich combination takes on a new personality when wrapped in a tortilla instead of bread. Try it in lavosh or pita bread, too.

1 pkg. (8 oz.) cream cheese, softened
1 tbs. finely chopped red bell pepper
1 tbs. finely chopped fresh chives
1 tbs. finely chopped green olives
6 medium flour tortillas

18 slices turkey
18 slices roast beef
18 leaves red lettuce, ribs removed
3 ripe Hass avocados, sliced

In a small bowl, combine cream cheese, red pepper, chives and olives and mix well. Lay tortillas on a work surface. Spread cheese mixture over tortillas, dividing evenly. Lay 3 thin slices of turkey, overlapping, across the center of each tortilla. Repeat layering with roast beef. Top with lettuce leaves and avocado slices, dividing evenly. Wrap fillings roll-up-style (see page 6) into a log and wrap tightly with plastic wrap; twist ends to secure. Refrigerate log for at least 1 hour. Remove log from refrigerator, remove plastic wrap and cut each log into 1½-inch slices. Serve on a platter.

LATIN ROAST PORK AND AVOCADO ROLL-UPS

These wonderful roll-ups will disappear quickly. Make them ahead of time so you can enjoy your party without fussing in the kitchen. Or, make them into wraps and cut in half for hearty servings. The pork will continue to cook a bit after it is taken out of the oven.

1 lb. boneless pork loin
3-4 tbs. *Latin Rub*, follows
3 tbs. prepared horseradish
1 pkg. (8 oz.) cream cheese, softened
¼ cup crushed pineapple, well drained

6 large flour tortillas
1 jar (8 oz.) roasted red bell peppers, drained
3 ripe Hass avocados, cut into thin slices
8 oz. alfalfa sprouts

Heat oven to 350°. Coat all surfaces of pork loin with *Latin Rub* and let stand in a shallow roasting pan for about 15 minutes. Place pork in oven and roast for about 45 minutes, or until the internal temperature registers 155° on a meat thermometer. Remove pork from oven and cool. Cut cooled pork roast into very thin slices.

In a small bowl, mix horseradish, cream cheese and pineapple until well blended. Lay tortillas on a work surface and spread with cream cheese mixture, dividing evenly. Top each tortilla with layers of pepper, avocado and sprouts, dividing evenly. Lay pork slices over sprouts. Wrap fillings roll-up-style (see page 6) into a log and wrap tightly with plastic wrap; twist ends to secure. Refrigerate log overnight. Remove log from refrigerator, remove plastic wrap and cut each log into 11/2-inch slices. Serve on a platter.

LATIN RUB

You can also use this seasoning on pork chops, ribs or roasts.

¼ cup ground cumin
¼ cup chili powder
2 tbs. ground coriander
1 tbs. cinnamon

1 tbs. brown sugar
2 tbs. salt
1 tbs. red pepper flakes
2 tbs. black pepper

Combine all ingredients in a jar with a tight-fitting lid and shake until well blended. Store at room temperature.

HOAGIE ROLL-UPS

This take-off on a Hoagie sandwich is a lunch-box favorite. Eat it as a sandwich or serve it cut into rounds for a casual get-together. Use your favorite sliced cheese. You can add thinly sliced vegetables of your choice if desired.

4 medium flour tortillas
mustard
mayonnaise
12 slices bologna

16 slices salami
8 slices American cheese
1 cup torn iceberg or romaine lettuce
4 Roma tomatoes, thinly sliced

Lay tortillas on a work surface. Spread ½ of each tortilla with mustard and remaining ½ with mayonnaise. Cover each tortilla with 3 slices bologna, 4 slices salami and 2 slices cheese, leaving a ½-inch border. Top cheese with lettuce and tomatoes, dividing evenly. Wrap fillings roll-up-style (see page 6) into a log and wrap tightly with plastic wrap; twist ends to secure. Refrigerate log for at least 1 hour. Pack whole in a lunch box. Or, remove plastic wrap, slice log into 1½-inch rounds and serve on a platter.

HIGH-ENERGY HAM AND VEGGIE ROLL-UPS

Makes 30 pieces

You needn't be a fancy cook to assemble this healthy roll-up. It is tasty with other types of meats, chicken and turkey, too.

6 medium flour tortillas, or 4 lavosh
2 tbs. hot mustard
1 cup shredded lettuce
4 thin slices ham
4 slices Swiss or other cheese
4 carrots, peeled and slivered
¼ cup mild or hot salsa
½ cup alfalfa sprouts

Lay tortillas on a work surface and spread with mustard. Top each tortilla with layers of lettuce, ham, cheese, carrots, salsa and sprouts, dividing evenly. Wrap fillings roll-up-style (see page 6) into a log and wrap tightly with waxed paper; twist ends to secure. Refrigerate log for at least 1 hour. Remove log from refrigerator, remove plastic wrap and cut each log into 1½-inch slices. Serve on a platter.

GREEK-INSPIRED MINI ROLL-UPS

Makes 40 pieces

This roll-up is a take-off of a Greek "gyro" sandwich. For variety, substitute thinly sliced roast beef or lamb for the pork, or your favorite cheese for the feta.

½ cup low-fat mayonnaise
½ cup plain yogurt, plus more for spreading
1 pkg. (1 oz.) taco seasoning mix
1 lb. cooked pork roast, very thinly sliced
8 medium flour tortillas, or 4 lavosh
1 cup shredded lettuce
4 tomatoes, diced
8 oz. feta cheese, crumbled

In a bowl, mix mayonnaise, ½ cup yogurt, taco seasoning and sliced meat. Lay tortillas on a work surface. Spread filling over ½ of each tortilla, leaving a 1-inch border at the edge. Top filling with layers of lettuce, tomatoes and cheese, dividing evenly. Spread yogurt along tortilla edges all the way around. Wrap fillings roll-up-style (see page 6) into a log and wrap tightly with waxed paper; twist ends to secure. Refrigerate log for at least 1 hour. Remove log from refrigerator, remove plastic wrap and cut each log into 1- to 1½-inch slices. Serve on a platter.

WRAPS AND ROLL-UPS WITH POULTRY

LET'S HAVE CHICKEN TONIGHT

These days, chicken is readily available in a variety of forms, both cooked and uncooked. For the perfect work-night meal, purchase cooked chicken from the deli and add a binder, a crunchy slaw and your choice of sauce and toss them into a wrap. Other types of poultry, such as turkey and duck, work well in wraps, too. Improvise with your favorite ingredients.

- Combine diced cooked chicken breast with black beans, cheddar cheese, barbecue sauce and a dollop of sour cream or guacamole. Wrap in a flour tortilla.
- Combine diced cooked chicken breast, Mandarin orange segments, roasted cashew nuts, chopped green onions, diced red bell pepper, alfalfa sprouts and mayonnaise mixed with a little lemon juice and sesame oil. Wrap in a spinach tortilla.
- Combine cooked turkey chunks with diced onion, sliced black olives, fresh cilantro and cream cheese mixed with chili sauce. Wrap in a chile tortilla.

CAESAR CHICKEN WRAPS

Wrap restaurants consistently report this as their most popular wrap combination. It's easy to assemble when you use prepared ingredients.

4 broiled or grilled chicken breast halves, cut into strips
½ tsp. salt
¼ tsp. pepper
½ tsp. ground cumin
4 cups torn crisp lettuce, bite-sized pieces
4 large plum or salad tomatoes, diced
½ cup *Zesty Caesar Dressing*, page 44, or use purchased
4 large whole wheat or spinach tortillas
½ cup grated Romano cheese

Place cooked chicken strips in a medium bowl and season with salt, pepper and cumin. Add lettuce, tomatoes and Caesar dressing and toss to combine. Lay tortillas on a work surface and divide chicken mixture among tortillas. Sprinkle with grated cheese. Wrap according to desired style on pages 4 to 6.

THAI CHICKEN WRAPS WITH PEANUT SAUCE

Piquant, pungent and pretty are good words to describe this quick-to-assemble combination. Purchase ready-made ingredients from the market or make the homemade elements in advance.

4 boneless chicken breast halves, grilled and coarsely chopped
½ cup *Chunky Mango Salsa*, page 48
½ cup *Thai Peanut Sauce*, page 43
1 bunch spinach, washed, patted dry and coarse stems removed
1 cup cooked *Curried Rice*, page 29 made with jasmine rice
4 large spinach tortillas, warmed
¼ cup sour cream

In a medium bowl, combine chicken, salsa and peanut sauce and mix well. In a skillet over high heat, cook spinach for 1 minute, until wilted. Add prepared rice to skillet and mix well.

Lay tortillas on a work surface. Divide chicken mixture among tortillas, dividing evenly. Top with rice mixture, dividing evenly. Top each wrap with 1 tbs. of the sour cream. Wrap according to desired style on pages 4 to 6.

FIESTA CHICKEN WRAPS

Makes 8

Adjust the "heat" of this dish by the selection of taco sauce and chile peppers.

1 tsp. vegetable oil
1 lb. boneless chicken breasts, cut into ¾-inch strips
½ cup prepared mild or hot taco sauce
1 cup sweet corn kernels
1½ cups cooked rice or quinoa (see page 29 or 35)
8 large flour tortillas, warmed
¾ cup sour cream
½ cup crumbled goat cheese
1 can (4 oz.) sliced jalapeño chiles or chopped green chiles, drained
Salsa Fresca, page 47, or use purchased

In a medium skillet, heat oil over medium-high heat and stir-fry chicken strips for about 3 minutes on each side, until no longer pink. Stir in taco sauce and corn, reduce heat to low and simmer gently for 3 to 4 minutes. Remove from heat and stir in quinoa.

Lay tortillas on a work surface. Divide filling mixture among tortillas. Top filling with sour cream, goat cheese and chiles, dividing evenly. Wrap according to desired style on pages 4 to 6. Serve salsa on the side.

MARINATED CHICKEN WRAPS
WITH MANGO-PEAR SALSA

These wraps are bursting with delicious flavors.

4 cloves garlic, minced

3-inch piece fresh ginger, peeled and
  chopped

¼ cup soy sauce

¼ cup lime juice

2 tbs. toasted sesame oil, optional

3 large boneless, skinless chicken breast
  halves

2 cups cooked jasmine or wild rice (page
  29) or orzo (page 34)

1 cup roasted sunflower kernels

½ cup thinly sliced celery

8 large flour tortillas, warmed

1 cup *Mango-Pear Salsa*, page 48

In a locking plastic bag, combine garlic, ginger, soy sauce, lime juice and sesame oil, if using. Add chicken breasts, seal bag and marinate for 2 hours in the refrigerator. Prepare a hot barbecue fire or heat broiler to high. Remove chicken from bag, pat dry and grill or broil for about 5 minutes per side, or until cooked through. Dice chicken and place in a large bowl with rice, sunflower kernels and celery.

Lay tortillas on a work surface. Divide filling mixture among tortillas and top with salsa, dividing evenly. Wrap according to desired style on pages 4 to 6.

TERIYAKI CHICKEN WRAPS

This recipe is also delicious made with turkey or beef.

1½ cups soy sauce
½ cup lemon juice
1¼ tsp. ground ginger
2 cloves garlic, minced
¼ cup minced Italian parsley
2 boneless chicken breast halves
1 cup uncooked jasmine rice

½ cup broccoli florets
½ cup chopped red bell pepper
1 can (5 oz.) water chestnuts, drained and
   sliced
1 cup bean sprouts
1 cup Chinese pea pods, cut into thirds
8 large flour or tomato tortillas, warmed

In a locking plastic bag, combine soy sauce, lemon juice, ginger, garlic and parsley. Add chicken breasts, seal bag and refrigerate overnight.

Drain chicken, reserving ½ cup of the marinade. Follow instructions for cooking rice on page 29, substituting ½ cup reserved marinade for ½ cup rice cooking liquid. Cut chicken into thin strips. In a skillet or wok over medium-high heat, stir-fry chicken for about 3 minutes on each side. Add broccoli, pepper, water chestnuts, bean sprouts and pea pods and stir-fry briefly. Remove from heat and stir in rice. Lay tortillas on a work surface. Divide filling among tortillas and wrap according to desired style on pages 4 to 6.

CURRIED CHICKEN AND FRUIT WRAPS

Makes 10–12

This elegant and easy wrap has a subtle curry-flavored dressing that helps blend the flavors.

2 cups diced cooked chicken
1 cup diced apples
1 cup sliced bananas
1 cup shredded coconut
1 cup blanched golden raisins
1 cup thinly sliced celery
1 cup pine nuts

1 cup *Plum Chutney*, page 67, or other fruit
  chutney
½ cup mayonnaise
1 tbs. lime or lemon juice
2 tbs. curry powder
10-12 large flour tortillas

In a large bowl, combine chicken, apples, bananas, coconut, raisins, celery, nuts and chutney and mix well. In another bowl, mix mayonnaise, lime juice and curry powder; add to chicken mixture and toss lightly. Cover bowl and refrigerate mixture overnight.

Remove chicken mixture from refrigerator about 1 hour before serving. When ready to serve, lay tortillas on a work surface. Divide filling among tortillas and wrap according to desired style on pages 4 to 6.

CHICKEN WRAPS WITH COUSCOUS
AND DRIED CRANBERRIES

Any one or a combination of dried fruit, such as cherries, raisins, prunes or apricots, can be substituted for the cranberries. From start to finish, this wrap should take only about 10 minutes to cook up.

1 tbs. vegetable oil or butter	½ cup dried cranberries
2 cups chicken strips	1 tbs. butter or margarine
1 cup chicken stock	1 cup instant couscous
¼ cup water	8 large flour tortillas, warmed

In a 4-quart saucepan, heat oil over medium-high heat and sauté chicken strips for about 3 minutes on each side, until no longer pink. Add chicken stock, water, dried cranberries and butter and bring to a boil over high heat. Stir in couscous, cover and remove from heat. Let stand for 5 minutes or until ready to serve. Fluff grains with a fork.

Lay tortillas on a work surface. Divide filling among tortillas and wrap according to desired style on pages 4 to 6.

SMOKED CHICKEN SALAD WRAPS

These spectacular wraps are great luncheon or dinner fare. For a different flavor, substitute crumbled goat cheese, ranchero cheese or feta cheese for the Monterey Jack. Purchase prepared smoked chicken from the deli or gourmet grocer. Or, use broiled or grilled chicken.

1½ lb. smoked chicken meat, diced

½ lb. Monterey Jack cheese, cut into long, narrow strips

1 cup chopped celery

1 red bell pepper, roasted, peeled, seeded and chopped

2 tbs. Dijon-style mustard

¾ cup mayonnaise

2 tbs. finely chopped Italian parsley or cilantro

2 tbs. finely chopped chives

1 tbs. lemon juice

8 large flour tortillas

8 medium leaves Bibb lettuce, torn into bite-sized pieces

2 large, ripe Hass avocados, peeled and thinly sliced

In a large bowl, combine chicken, cheese, celery, bell pepper, mustard, ½ cup of the mayonnaise, parsley, chives and lemon juice and toss well.

Lay tortillas on a work surface and spread with remaining ¼ cup mayonnaise. Divide lettuce and chicken mixture among tortillas. Top with avocado slices, dividing evenly. Wrap according to desired style on pages 4 to 6.

CHICKEN WRAPS WITH POTATOES AND RICE

Makes 8–10

A flavor combination popular in New Mexico inspired this gourmet burrito adaptation.

1½ lb. small red potatoes, halved
¼ cup olive oil
2 tbs. chopped fresh cilantro
1½ tsp. garlic powder
1½ tsp onion powder
4 boneless chicken breast halves
½ cup light soy sauce
½ cup water

2 tbs. Dijon-style mustard
½ tsp. ground cumin
½ can (4 oz. can) chopped green chiles, or more to taste
2 cups *Southwestern Rice*, page 31
1 cup shredded carrots
½ cup thinly sliced green bell pepper
8-10 large flour or spinach tortillas, warmed

Heat oven to 400°. In a 2-quart baking dish, toss potatoes with olive oil. Add cilantro, garlic powder, onion powder and chicken and mix well. In a small bowl, mix soy sauce, water, mustard, cumin and green chiles and spoon over chicken and potatoes. Cover dish tightly with aluminum foil and bake for 20 to 25 minutes, until chicken is cooked through; cool slightly.

Dice chicken and potatoes into ½-inch cubes and place in large bowl. Add rice, carrots, and green pepper and mix lightly. Lay tortillas on a work surface. Divide filling among tortillas and wrap according to desired style on pages 4 to 6.

FRUITY CHICKEN WRAPS WITH COUSCOUS

Makes 6

Try this with rice, couscous or a combination. For added flavor, substitute orange juice for ½ of the water in the rice or couscous.

2 tsp. vegetable oil
4-6 boneless skinless chicken halves (about 2 lb.), cut into thin strips
½ cup whole-berry cranberry sauce
½ cup chili sauce
2 tbs. orange marmalade

½ tsp. pumpkin pie spice
¼ cup raisins
6 large flour tortillas, warmed
6-12 romaine lettuce leaves
3 cups *Orange Couscous*, page 33
3 cups *Cole Slaw Vinaigrette*, page 40

In a skillet, heat oil over medium-high heat and saute chicken for about 8 minutes, drain fat. In a small bowl, combine cranberry sauce, chili sauce, marmalade and pumpkin pie spice and pour over chicken. Simmer over low heat for about 5 minutes, until chicken is cooked and sauce thickens. Add raisins during the last few minutes.

Lay tortillas on a work surface and place 1 to 2 lettuce leaves on each tortilla. Top lettuce with layers of chicken mixture, couscous and cole slaw, dividing evenly. Wrap according to desired style on pages 4 to 6.

DUCK WRAPS WITH BEANS AND WILD RICE

Makes 8–10

Look for duck in specialty food stores or at a butcher shop. Duck breasts are convenient and flavorful to use, but you can also use the leftovers from a whole roasted duck. Or, save enough for a "doggie bag" after ordering a Peking duck in a Chinese restaurant. Tomatillos are small green fruits that resemble tomatoes, but they're wrapped in a brown papery husk. Remove the husk and wash them well before using.

1 small onion, finely chopped
1 cup cooked black beans
1 cup sweet corn kernels
2 tomatillos, chopped
1 tsp. Tabasco Sauce
2 cups cooked wild rice (see *Basic Rice*, page 29)

2 cups shredded cooked duck meat
8-10 large flour tortillas, warmed
1 cup sour cream
1 cup mixed shredded Monterey Jack, mozzarella and/or cheddar cheese
1 cup shredded lettuce

In a medium bowl, mix together onion, beans, corn, tomatillos and Tabasco. Add rice and duck meat and mix well.

Lay tortillas on a work surface. Divide duck mixture among tortillas. Top with layers of sour cream, cheese and lettuce, dividing evenly. Wrap according to desired style on pages 4 to 6.

TURKEY, SWEET POTATO
AND CRANBERRY WRAPS

Makes 4

Don't relegate the use of these Thanksgiving-style foods to once per year. Keep the fixings on hand for lunches and quick meals.

1 large orange-fleshed sweet potato, peeled
   and cut into uniform chunks
¼ cup orange juice
1 tbs. butter
salt to taste
1 cup diced cooked turkey

1 cup whole-berry cranberry sauce
½ cup chopped fresh celery
½ cup chopped green bell pepper
½ cup walnut pieces, optional
4 large flour tortillas, warmed

In a saucepan, cook sweet potatoes in boiling water until tender. Drain and let stand for about 5 minutes. Place potatoes in a bowl and mash with orange juice, butter and salt. In another bowl, mix turkey, cranberry sauce, celery, bell peppers and walnuts, if using.

Lay tortillas on a work surface. Divide sweet potato and turkey mixtures among tortillas and wrap according to desired style on pages 4 to 6.

HOLIDAY HOLDOVER WRAPS

Makes 5–6

Here is a delicious combination that can be varied depending on what is left over from a holiday meal. This one pulls together Thanksgiving trimmings with color, crunch and sweetness. It is as good with slivers of roast beef, pork or chicken as it is with turkey.

5–6 large flour or spinach tortillas, warmed
3 cups *Classic Cole Slaw*, page 40
Thai Peanut Sauce, page 43
romaine lettuce leaves
1 cup prepared mashed sweet potatoes
½ cucumber, peeled and cut into long thin strips
1½ cups cooked turkey strips

Lay tortillas on a work surface. Mix cole slaw with peanut sauce and drain excess liquid. Place 1 to 2 lettuce leaves on each tortilla. Top lettuce with layers of slaw, sweet potatoes, cucumber and turkey strips. Wrap according to desired style on pages 4 to 6.

TURKEY, CRANBERRY AND APPLE ROLL-UPS

Makes 40 pieces

This combination is hard to beat for color and flavor. Stack the sliced roll-ups on a tray and watch them disappear. For variety, add Swiss or other cheeses to the layers. If using lavosh, the ingredients will be divided differently.

5 red apples, thinly sliced
2 tbs. lemon juice
8 medium flour tortillas, or 4 lavosh
2 pkg. (8 oz. each) cream cheese, softened
1 can (16 oz.) whole-berry cranberry sauce
24 thin slices honey-roasted turkey
16 large leaves red lettuce, ribs removed

Place apples in a bowl and sprinkle with lemon juice to prevent browning. Lay tortillas on a work surface and spread with cream cheese. Carefully spread ½ of the cranberry sauce over cream cheese. Lay 3 slices turkey on each tortilla and carefully spread with remaining cranberry sauce. Top with apple slices, followed by lettuce leaves. Wrap fillings roll-up-style (see page 6) into a log and wrap tightly with plastic wrap; twist ends to secure. Refrigerate log for 2 hours or overnight. Remove log from refrigerator, remove plastic wrap and cut each log into 1½-inch slices. Serve on a platter.

CALIFORNIA-STYLE ROLL-UPS

California has earned a reputation for being health-conscious and trend-setting; this roll-up is a good example.

6 medium flour tortillas, or 4 lavosh
3 tbs. grainy mustard
12 leaves Bibb or romaine lettuce, ribs removed
18 thin slices smoked turkey
12 slices Monterey Jack or mozzarella cheese, or a combination, cut into ½-inch strips
1½ cups *Mild Guacamole*, page 53, or *Spicy Hot Guacamole*, page 54
1 cup clover or other sprouts

Lay tortillas on a work surface and spread each with ½ tbs. of the mustard. Place 2 lettuce leaves on each tortilla. Top lettuce with layers of turkey, cheese and guacamole, dividing evenly. Top with sprouts. Wrap fillings roll-up-style (see page 6) into a log and wrap tightly with plastic wrap; twist ends to secure. Refrigerate log for 2 hours or overnight. Remove log from refrigerator, remove plastic wrap and cut each log into 1½ inch slices.

CAESAR TURKEY ROLL-UPS

Thinly slice these roll-ups for appetizers or into larger portions for a full meal.

4 lavosh, or 6 medium flour tortillas
¾ cup purchased thick Caesar salad dressing
12 leaves romaine lettuce, ribs removed
2 cups finely diced cooked turkey
1 jar (7 oz.) roasted red bell peppers, drained
½ cup grated Parmesan cheese

Lay lavosh on a work surface and spread with dressing. Place 3 romaine lettuce leaves on each lavosh, flattening gently. Place turkey on ½ of each lavosh, dividing evenly. Top with layers of roasted red peppers and sprinkle with Parmesan cheese. Wrap fillings roll-up-style (see page 6) into a log and cover tightly with plastic wrap; twist ends to secure. Refrigerate log for up to 1 hour. Remove log from refrigerator, remove waxed paper and cut each log into 1½-inch appetizer rounds or into halves or quarters.

WRAPS AND ROLL-UPS WITH FISH AND SHELLFISH

Wraps and roll-ups made with fish and shellfish lend themselves to fancier presentations than some of the other types in this book. The binders and sauces should be subtly flavored, so they won't compete with the delicate flavors of the seafood. Note that everything need not be prepared the day you eat it. Leftover grilled salmon or extra boiled shrimp are perfect choices for stuffing into tomorrow's lunch wrap.

- Combine barbecued shrimp with chopped tomato, minced red onion, chopped fresh cilantro, chopped serrano or jalapeño chiles, jasmine rice and chili sauce. Wrap in a tomato tortilla.

- Combine cubes of marinated, grilled swordfish with diced Roma tomato, diced red onion, fresh oregano, rice and mild fish sauce. Wrap in a sun-dried tomato tortilla.

- Combine pieces of snapper, romaine lettuce, red bell pepper, jasmine rice, sour cream and pesto-tomato salsa. Wrap in a spinach tortilla.

CAJUN SCALLOP AND PEPPER WRAPS

Makes 4

You can use any kind of fish in this wrap instead of, or in addition to, scallops.

1½ cups *Classic Cole Slaw*, page 40
1 tsp. ground ginger
¼ cup chopped green onions
1 red bell pepper, seeded, ribs removed and cut into slivers
1 cup sour cream
1 tbs. olive or vegetable oil
1½ lb. bay scallops
4 large sun-dried tomato tortillas
1 cup cooked basmati rice, see page 29
½ cup purchased salsa

Place cole slaw in a medium bowl and stir in ginger, green onions, red pepper and sour cream; set aside. In a medium skillet, heat oil over medium-high heat. Add scallops and sauté for about 2 to 3 minutes, turning often, until just opaque.

Lay tortillas on a work surface. Layer rice, cole slaw, scallops and salsa on tortillas, dividing evenly. Wrap according to desired style on pages 4 to 6.

SALMON WRAPS WITH DILL SAUCE

Freshly cooked salmon is ideal for this recipe, but canned salmon yields tasty results, too.

2 lb. salmon fillets, broiled or grilled, or 2
   cans (14½ oz. each) salmon, broken up
   with a fork
juice of 1 lemon
1 cup Thousand Island salad dressing
1 cup nonfat plain yogurt
½ cup sweet pickle relish
1 tsp. Dijon-style mustard
1 cup thinly sliced celery

½ cup thinly sliced green onions
½ cup chopped red bell pepper
3 tbs. chopped fresh dill
½ cup pine nuts
2 cups cooked jasmine rice, see page 29
½ tsp. pepper
8 large flour or tomato tortillas
1 cup shredded lettuce

Remove skin and any small bones from broiled salmon and break salmon into pieces. Place salmon in a bowl and toss with lemon juice. In another bowl, mix salad dressing, yogurt, pickle relish, mustard, celery, onions, bell pepper, dill and nuts. Stir in rice and pepper. Add salmon and mix gently.

Lay tortillas on a work surface. Divide filling among tortillas and top with lettuce. Wrap according to desired style on pages 4 to 6.

THAI-STYLE CURRIED SHRIMP WRAPS

Makes 6–8

For a delicious variation of these wraps, substitute chicken for the shrimp.

¼ cup diced red onion
½ cup chopped red bell pepper
½ cup shredded red cabbage
1 tbs. minced jalapeño chile
½ cup chopped celery
Peanut-Curry-Ginger Sauce, page 57

½ cup roasted unsalted peanuts
1 lb. medium shrimp, cooked, peeled,
   deveined and cut in half
2 cups cooked jasmine rice (see page 29),
   cooled
6–8 large flour or tomato tortillas, warmed

In a large bowl, mix onion, bell pepper, cabbage, jalapeño and celery. Add *Peanut-Curry-Ginger Sauce* and toss well. Add peanuts and shrimp and mix lightly. Cover and refrigerate for at least 1 hour.

Remove vegetable-shrimp mixture from refrigerator and mix with rice. Lay tortillas on a work surface and divide filling among tortillas. Wrap according to desired style on pages 4 to 6.

GARLIC SEAFOOD WRAPS

Use all three varieties of seafood, or any combination you prefer.

½ lb. cooked crabmeat, flaked
½ lb. cooked lobster meat, flaked
½ lb. large shrimp, cooked, peeled,
  deveined and cut into thirds
¼ cup mayonnaise
¼ cup sour cream
2 cloves garlic, minced

1 tbs. lemon juice
½ tsp. grated fresh lemon peel (zest)
1½ tsp. chopped fresh dill
1 tbs. Dijon-style mustard
dash hot pepper or Worcestershire sauce
8-10 large flour tortillas, warmed
3 cups *Classic Cole Slaw*, page 40

In a large bowl, mix crabmeat, lobster meat and shrimp. Add mayonnaise, sour cream, garlic, lemon juice, lemon peel, dill, mustard and hot pepper sauce and mix well.

Lay tortillas on a work surface. Divide seafood mixture among tortillas and top with cole slaw. Wrap according to desired style on pages 4 to 6.

LOX AND PIMIENTO
CREAM CHEESE ROLL-UPS

Looking for a different brunch idea? Here's a delicious variation of the lox-on-a-bagel standard.

1 pkg. (16 oz.) cream cheese, softened
1 jar (4 oz.) pimientos, drained and patted
   dry
1 can (8 oz.) sliced black olives, drained
   and patted dry

4 lavosh
12 oz. lox, thinly sliced
6 firm ripe Roma tomatoes, thinly sliced
1 white onion, very thinly sliced
16 leaves Bibb lettuce, patted dry

In a bowl, mix cream cheese, pimentos and olives until blended. Lay lavosh on a work surface and spread with cream cheese mixture. Divide lox among lavosh, overlapping slightly. Place layers of tomato, onion and lettuce leaves on lox, dividing evenly. Wrap fillings roll-up-style (see page 6) into a log and wrap tightly with plastic wrap; twist ends to secure. Refrigerate log for at least 1 hour. Remove log from refrigerator, remove plastic wrap and cut each log into 11/2-inch rounds. Serve on a platter.

WRAPS AND ROLL-UPS FOR DESSERT

FINISH WITH FLAIR

The same tortillas, lavosh and pita wrappers that you use to make savory wraps and roll-ups can be adapted inventively to dessert-style treats. Fruit-flavored and chocolate tortillas are perfect for your sweet concoctions, but flour tortillas work well, too. Once you get the hang of making dessert wraps, you can create your own concoctions with confidence.

- Combine ¾ cup cottage cheese with 2 tbs. sugar and ¼ tsp. each of grated fresh lemon peel (zest) and ground cardamom or cinnamon. Wrap envelope-style (see page 4) in a flour tortilla and sauté in butter until golden brown on both sides. Top with strawberry or other fruit preserves and a spoonful of sour cream.

- Top a heated dessert-flavored tortilla with fruit-flavored preserves, chopped walnuts, raisins and whipped cream. Fold tortilla dainty eater-style (see page 6), place on a plate and sprinkle with cinnamon.

- Spread a strawberry tortilla with softened cream cheese and top with diced seasonal fruits. Sprinkle with cinnamon and chopped walnuts and roll up dainty eater-style (see page 6). Let stand for 5 minutes. Garnish with whipped cream and additional chopped walnuts.

CURRIED FRUIT WRAPS

Top off a simple dinner dramatically with pineapple, raisins, coconut and curried rice wrapped in a flavored tortilla.

2 cups hot cooked *Curried Rice*, page 29
½ cup raisins
1 can (12 oz.) pineapple chunks, drained
½ cup shredded coconut
6 large strawberry tortillas or other fruit-flavored tortillas, warmed

As soon as rice finishes cooking, remove from heat and add raisins, pineapple and coconut to pan; do not mix. Cover pan and let stand for about 10 minutes. Uncover pan and stir rice and fruit until well blended.

Lay tortillas on a work surface and divide rice mixture among tortillas. Wrap dainty eater-style (see page 6).

YOGURT-FILLED ROLL-UPS

For a dramatic presentation, drizzle a little sauce around the serving plate and swirl it with a fork from the edges toward the center. Place the wrap in the middle of the dish and pour additional sauce over the top.

2 medium flour tortillas
butter-flavored cooking spray
2 tbs. cinnamon
¼ cup sugar
1 tbs. unsweetened cocoa powder

1 egg white
10 oz. vanilla or fruit-flavored yogurt
Chocolate Sauce or *Coffee-Chocolate Sauce*, follows

Heat oven to 350°. Lay tortillas on a work surface and spray with butter-flavored spray. In a small bowl, mix cinnamon, sugar and cocoa powder and sprinkle evenly on tortillas. Cut each tortilla into quarters and roll each piece from the pointed end to the wide end over the handle of a wooden spoon to make a cylinder. Brush the pointed end with egg white, press to seal and place cylinder on a baking pan seam-side down. Remove spoon and repeat process with remaining tortillas. Bake for 10 minutes and cool. Spoon yogurt into the centers of cylinders. Place 1 to 2 roll-ups on each serving plate and drizzle with *Chocolate Sauce* or *Coffee Chocolate Sauce.*

CHOCOLATE SAUCE

Makes 1½ cups

To reheat this sauce after cooling, set the jar without the lid in a pan of warm water or heat in a microwave until desired consistency.

4 oz. unsweetened chocolate, chopped
¾ cup boiling water

1¼ cups sugar
1 tsp. vanilla extract

In a saucepan, combine chocolate and boiling water over medium-low heat and stir until chocolate is completely melted. Stir in sugar and increase heat until mixture barely simmers. Cook, stirring, for 5 minutes. Remove from heat and stir in vanilla. To store, pour into a covered jar and refrigerate.

COFFEE-CHOCOLATE SAUCE

Makes 1½ cups

A touch of coffee greatly enhances this basic chocolate sauce.

4 oz. unsweetened chocolate, chopped
¼ cup light corn syrup
¼ cup heavy cream

2 tbs. butter or margarine
¼ cup sugar
¼ cup coffee liqueur, such as Kahlua

In the top of double boiler, combine ingredients and cook over simmering water, stirring constantly, for 10 minutes. Remove from heat and stir in liqueur. To store, pour into a covered jar and refrigerate.

LOW-FAT STRAWBERRY CHIMICHANGAS

Fruit preserves and fresh fruit fill these oven-baked Mexican-style turnovers. Use fresh, frozen or canned fruits, but be sure to drain frozen or canned fruits well.

2 tsp. berry-flavored liqueur
2–3 tsp. cornstarch
¼ cup strawberry or other berry preserves
1 tsp. orange marmalade or grated fresh
    orange peel (zest)

2 cups chopped strawberries, blueberries or
    pitted sweet cherries
6 medium flour tortillas
¼ cup nonfat milk
1 tbs. cinnamon mixed with 1/4 cup sugar

Heat oven to 500°. In a medium bowl, mix liqueur with 2 tsp. cornstarch (3 tsp. if using frozen fruit), preserves, marmalade and strawberries. Lay tortillas on a work surface and brush both sides of each tortilla liberally with milk; let stand for about 1 minute, until tortillas are soft. Divide filling among tortillas and wrap fillings envelope-style (see page 4). Place wraps on an oiled baking sheet, seam-side down. Brush tops of wraps with milk and bake until golden brown, about 8 to 10 minutes, brushing with milk every 3 minutes. Cool slightly and dust with cinnamon-sugar mixture.

CHOCOLATE-BANANA ROLL-UPS

A take-off on a Mexican chimichanga makes a deliciously decadent dessert.

4 medium flour, strawberry or other dessert-flavored tortillas
¼ cup chocolate-nut spread, such as Nutella, or 1 cup chocolate chips, melted
1 egg white, optional
3 large ripe bananas, sliced
1 tbs. peanut oil
ice cream or whipped cream
fresh mint leaves for garnish, optional
Chocolate Sauce, page 145, or use purchased, optional

Lay tortillas on a work surface and spread with chocolate spread. Top spread with sliced bananas, dividing evenly. Wrap fillings loosely roll-up-style into a log (see page 6). Brush edges of tortillas with a thin coat of water or egg white and press to form a seal. In a large skillet or wok, heat oil over medium-high heat. Place filled tortillas in pan, seam-side down. Cook until lightly browned on all sides. Serve warm on plate with ice cream or whipped topping. Garnish with mint leaves or *Chocolate Sauce*.

NUTTY-FRUITY RICE ROLL-UPS

Makes 12–28 pieces

Serve pieces on individual dessert plates and with fruit sauce and a spoonful of whipped cream or dessert topping. For a fancier presentation, drizzle the colorful fruit sauce on the dish and swirl it with a fork. Place roll-ups on top, drizzle with additional sauce and top with whipped cream.

1 cup uncooked basmati or long-grain white rice
½ cup orange juice
1½ cups water
1 large Granny Smith apple, diced
1 large Red Delicious apple, diced
1 tbs. lemon juice
½ cup raisins
½ cup chopped walnuts
6 medium cinnamon-apple, strawberry or other fruit-flavored tortillas
½ cup strawberry preserves
½ tsp. cinnamon
Fruit Sauce, follows
whipped cream or dessert topping

In a saucepan, bring rice, orange juice and water to a boil. Reduce heat to very low, cover and simmer for about 15 minutes, until all liquid is absorbed. In a medium bowl, mix apples with lemon juice. Stir in raisins and walnuts.

Lay tortillas on a work surface and place rice in a line along the center of each tortilla, dividing evenly. Carefully spread rice with strawberry preserves and sprinkle with cinnamon. Top with apple mixture. Wrap fillings roll-up-style into a log (see page 6). Cut each log in halves or thirds. Serve with Fruit Sauce and whipped cream.

FRUIT SAUCE   Makes about 2½ cups

Look for the fruit juice with the ice cream toppings or jams and jellies in the supermarket.

1 cup unsweetened cherry, strawberry or blueberry juice
½–¾ cups sugar
1 tbs. cornstarch mixed with a small amount of water

2 tsp. lemon juice
1 cup crushed cherries, strawberries or blueberries
2 tbs. sherry, white wine or liqueur

In the top of a double boiler, combine fruit juice and sugar; heat over boiling water until just at the boiling point. Add cornstarch mixture and cook, stirring, until thick and clear. Remove from heat and stir in lemon juice; cool. Stir in fruit and sherry. Serve hot or cold.

MANGO-CRANBERRY DESSERT WRAPS

Sweet and tart flavors combine in this tasty dessert wrap.

4 medium flour tortillas, or 2 lavosh
3 oz. cream cheese, softened
½ cup mango jelly
⅔ cup whole-berry cranberry sauce
½ cup coarsely chopped walnuts

Lay tortillas on a work surface and spread with cream cheese. Top with layers of chutney and cranberry sauce, dividing evenly and spreading carefully. Sprinkle with nuts. Wrap fillings dainty eater-style (see page 6) and serve whole or cut into halves.

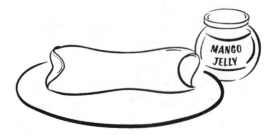

MARMALADE ROLL-UPS

There's no need to stand over a hot griddle and make pancakes when you can substitute ready-made flavored tortillas. Serve these with hot syrup for a weekend breakfast treat or fast dessert.

4–6 medium strawberry or cinnamon-apple tortillas, warmed
1 cup orange marmalade
warmed maple syrup

Lay tortillas on a work surface and spread with marmalade. Wrap filling roll-up-style into a log (see page 6). Serve 1 to 2 roll-ups per person with a small pitcher of warm maple syrup.

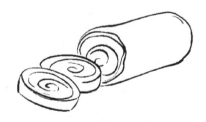

INDEX

Serve Creative, Easy, Nutritious Meals with **nitty gritty**® Cookbooks

1 or 2, Cooking for
100 Dynamite Desserts
9 x 13 Pan Cookbook
Bagels, Best
Barbecue Cookbook
Beer and Good Food
Big Book of Bread Machine Recipes
Big Book of Kitchen Appliance Recipes
Big Book of Snacks and Appetizers
Blender Drinks
Bread Baking
Bread Machine
Bread Machine II
Bread Machine III
Bread Machine V
Bread Machine VI
Bread Machine, Entrees
Burger Bible
Cappuccino/Espresso
Casseroles
Chicken, Unbeatable
Chile Peppers
Clay, Cooking in

Coffee and Tea
Convection Oven
Cook-Ahead Cookbook
Crockery Pot, Extra-Special
Deep Fryer
Dehydrator Cookbook
Edible Gifts
Edible Pockets
Fabulous Fiber Cookery
Fondue and Hot Dips
Fondue, New International
Freezer, 'Fridge, Pantry
Garlic Cookbook
Grains, Cooking with
Healthy Cooking on Run
Ice Cream Maker
Indoor Grill, Cooking on
Italian Recipes, Quick and Easy
Juicer Book II
Kids, Cooking with Your
Kids, Healthy Snacks for
Loaf Pan, Recipes for
Low-Carb Recipes

Lowfat American
No Salt No Sugar No Fat   (REVISED)
Party Foods/Appetizers
Pasta Machine Cookbook
Pasta, Quick and Easy
Pinch of Time
Pizza, Best
Porcelain, Cooking in
Pressure Cooker, Recipes (REVISED)
Rice Cooker
Rotisserie Oven Cooking
Sandwich Maker
Simple Substitutions
Skillet, Sensational
Slow Cooking
Slow Cooker, Vegetarian
Soups and Stews
Soy & Tofu Recipes
Tapas Fantásticas
Toaster Oven Cookbook
Waffles & Pizzelles
Wedding Catering Cookbook
Wraps and Roll-Ups   (REVISED)

For a free catalog, call: Bristol Publishing Enterprises
(800) 346-4889
www.bristolpublishing.com